GEORGE STEVENS

INTERVIEWS

CONVERSATIONS WITH FILMMAKERS SERIES
PETER BRUNETTE, GENERAL EDITOR

Photo credit: Photofest

GEORGE STEVENS

INTERVIEWS

EDITED BY PAUL CRONIN

UNIVERSITY PRESS OF MISSISSIPPI / JACKSON

www.upress.state.ms.us

The University Press of Mississippi is a member of
the Association of American University Presses.

Manufactured in the United States of America

12 11 10 09 08 07 06 05 04 4 3 2 1

∞

Library of Congress Cataloging-in-Publication Data

Stevens, George Cooper, 1904–
George Stevens : interviews / edited by Paul Cronin.
p. cm.
Includes index.
Filmography:
ISBN 1-57806-638-7 (alk. paper)—ISBN 1-57806-639-5 (pbk. : alk. paper)
1. Stevens, George Cooper, 1904– —Interviews. 2. Motion picture producers
and directors—United States—Interviews. I. Cronin, Paul. II. Title.

PN1998.3.S738A3 2004
791.4302′33′092—dc22 2003022742

British Library Cataloging-in-Publication Data available

CONTENTS

INTRODUCTION

At first glance, George Stevens appears to be the quintessential Hollywood director. But a closer look at his achievements shows him to be more than just the creator of some of the smartest melodramas and comedies of the 1930s and 1940s, and several of the most important and enduring dramas of postwar American cinema. As a leading producer/director of his era, Stevens repeatedly pushed against the Hollywood grain, and nearly twenty-five years after his death, his achievements remain largely unexplored.

A man of the West—he was born in Oakland, California—Stevens started work in his parents' West Coast touring stock theater company as a child actor and stage manager. At the point when it became clear that cinema was replacing live theater as the American public's entertainment of choice, Landers and Georgie Cooper Stevens moved south to Los Angeles with their two sons, Jack and George. Stevens's formal education was abandoned soon thereafter (though intelligent and well-read, his spelling was never good), in part because he spent much of his time driving his actor father to auditions at nearby Hollywood studios. It was here where Stevens, at the age of only seventeen, became an assistant cameraman, cutting his teeth on a series of Westerns produced by Hal Roach, many of which featured real cowboys. As James Silke explains in the introduction to his 1964 interview included in this volume, "The city boy went outdoors and learned to ride, rope and climb mountains. The young Stevens thrived on the new life and experiences that opened up for him to explore."

Within three years Stevens, who trained under the tutelage of cinematographer Floyd Jackman, had started work on the first of dozens of Laurel and Hardy shorts as a cameraman and gagman (he also shot many of the *Our Gang* and Harry Langdon comedies). After having solved the problem of Stan Laurel's blue eyes which did not adequately register on orthochromatic film stock (Stevens suggested panchromatic film be used instead), Roach decided to give the enterprising young man his first opportunity to direct. The result was the 1930 short *Ladies Last.* After moving first to Universal, and then to RKO in 1933, Stevens started work on a series of highly regarded light-hearted feature entertainments. Jumping from genre to genre, his films of this era include *Alice Adams*, featuring an important early role for Katharine Hepburn (who described Stevens as "a really brilliant director"), *Swing Time*, perhaps the most highly regarded Fred Astaire and Ginger Rogers musical, and the classic action adventure yarn *Gunga Din*, the influence of which can be seen on more than one recent Hollywood blockbuster.

By 1943 Stevens also had *Woman of the Year*, the first Hepburn and Spencer Tracy pairing, one that set the style and tone of the eight further films they made together, and the Cary Grant comedy *The Talk of the Town* under his belt. He had become, in the space of only ten years, one of America's most important and admired directors, having produced a stylish and diverse body of work that would foreshadow his postwar achievements. Then, at the age of nearly forty (well over draft age), Stevens left Hollywood for Europe, where he traveled with Allied forces from D-Day through to the battle for Berlin as the commander of a group of writers and cameramen (which included William Saroyan, Irwin Shaw, Ivan Moffat, who worked on the script *Giant*, and William Mellor, who would win Oscars shooting *A Place in the Sun* and *The Diary of Anne Frank*). Using his own 16 mm camera, Stevens shot important color sequences at the liberation of Paris, the meeting of Russian and American troops at Germany's river Elbe in April 1945, and the entry of American troops into Dachau concentration camp in southern Germany. As several of the conversations in this book make clear, Stevens's wartime experiences had a profound effect on him. "It must have changed my outlook entirely," he told James Silke in 1964. "Films were very much less important to me."

Consequently, Stevens's films underwent something of a sea change on his return from Europe. Between 1951 and 1956 he produced his "American Trilogy," three films that are more sober and, as several critics have suggested, thought-provoking than the prewar work. *A Place in the Sun* (which, writes Donald Richie, expresses the "attitude of the mature artist"), *Shane* (a film that Edward Countryman and Evonne von Heussen-Countryman note "considers violence where there is no law, both in terms of what a shooting does and as a historical problem in America's development"), and *Giant* (the epic that, as critic Richard Schickel noted recently, caused many to think differently about America's racial problems) solidified Stevens's international reputation as a director of quality American drama. His final films, which include *The Diary of Anne Frank*, certainly influenced by his experiences at Dachau, and *The Greatest Story Ever Told*, a retelling of the life of Jesus, were a fitting end to a career during which he earned two Academy Awards for Best Director, and numerous other nominations and awards.

His training at the hands of figures like Jackman and Laurel (the creative force behind the comic duo) meant that by the time Stevens was given the opportunity to direct himself, he had a wealth of technical experience to draw from. Edgardo Cozarinsky has written that Stevens "can be seen 'doing something' with every scene of his major films." Yet nearly thirty years after his death, Stevens remains a relatively ignored figure in American film history, and even though many cinemagoers know his work, most would be hard pushed to name the director of *Shane* or *Giant*. One reason for this is perhaps due to a certain snobbishness on the part of film scholars. Unlike figures such as Nicholas Ray, Alfred Hitchcock, and Howard Hawks, Stevens was never heralded as an *auteur* and paraded across the pages of French film magazines in the 1950s and '60s by the critics of that country. But in several crucial respects, Stevens—a director who rarely accepted studio assignments, preferring instead to initiate projects himself—can certainly be considered as the "author" of his films.

A look at his body of work reveals Stevens's filmmaking strategy over his forty-year career: quality over quantity. Unlike many of his Hollywood contemporaries, some of whom produced a film a year (and sometimes even more than that), Stevens always spent lengthy periods of preproduction working with writers on the screenplays of his films, a process that can be documented as early as *Alice Adams* in 1935. As Stevens tells Mary Ann Fisher in her 1963 interview, "For me it's absolutely necessary to start from the very beginning. I can't think of coming and contributing something anywhere along the line other than the very start. . . . The 'auteur' concept is certainly the most desirable form of film-making, from my point of view." Antonio Vellani, associate producer of *The Greatest Story Ever Told*, was present at numerous script conferences over a period of several years. For Vellani, Stevens "was primarily a writer, with an extraordinary control of the craft of screenwriting." In fact, as Stevens's interview at the American Film Institute with James Silke makes clear, on at least one film he was scripting at the same time as shooting, injecting a vibrant improvisatory nature to some of his work (an influence, perhaps, from his work with Laurel and Hardy), though as Edward Countryman and Evonne von Heussen-Countryman make clear, this was "much more the product of knowing where he wanted to take the film before he started shooting than of simply making it up as he went along."

As well as contributing immeasurably to the writing process, Stevens also did extensive historical research for many of his films during preproduction. "I've always been of the opinion that a director should never touch a film without having a basic knowledge of its contents," he explained to William Kirschner in 1963. As such, Stevens worked with a former member of the Dutch resistance during preproduction, and spent considerable time with Otto Frank, father of Anne, in the Amsterdam apartment where the Frank family hid from the Nazis, all to ensure that *The Diary of Anne Frank* was as true to reality as possible. When working on *The Greatest Story Ever Told*, Stevens appreciated the enormous responsibility involved in his subject matter. As a consequence, he spent three years researching the historical and religious background to the story before shooting a single foot of film, a process that included lengthy visits to Israel and Jordan in 1960. Stevens even hired an old-time cowhand as technical advisor for *Shane* who gave notes about everything from the costumes and eating habits of the characters, to the way they spoke. "I believe that if you make a film properly today, it'll be watched by people in fifty years time," George Stevens Jr. remembers his father telling him.

More evidence for Stevens's authorial status comes from the fact that he was vehement that the director retain absolute control of his work and be able to affect every element of a film's production. Always anxious to assert his rights as a director, something he did no matter whose feathers were ruffled in the process, Stevens never hesitated to ensure he had everything needed to construct precisely the film he wanted. Much to the chagrin of the studios, his shooting technique—the result of what has been called his "laborious perfectionism"—was to obtain coverage of a scene from every conceivable angle. As William Mellor noted, this meant that Stevens's cutting rooms were full of "about three times the usual amount of film." But it also gave him as many options as possible when editing, a process he was usually at the center of. Stevens's friend, the director Joseph Mankiewicz, explains that "after the actors were gone, the technicians were gone, there was nothing left but George and his film. It always seemed to me that the editing room was where George made his films. I don't know any other director that worked quite that way. And that's why the making of films, I thought, for George was a very private, personal thing."

At one point during production on *Shane* he was requested by the Production Code Administration to tone down the killing of Torrey (Elisha Cook Jr.). Stevens gave his audience no quarter by rigging Cook Jr. up to a block and pulley system, which meant that when hit by the bullet from Jack Wilson's gun, his entire body flew backwards into the mud. For Stevens, the scene played a crucial role within the story as a whole, intimately linked to what he talks to both Robert Hughes and Joe Hyams about in their conversations included here. "You know, the one thing I wanted to do with *Shane*," he explains to Hughes, "was to show if you point a .45 at a man and pull the trigger, you destroy an upright figure." Needless to say, Stevens—a man who cared passionately about the emotive and moral power of the stories he was telling—ensured that the scene passed the censors' eyes without alteration.

Moreover, Stevens was one of the first major producer/directors in Hollywood. His contract with Liberty Films, the company he established in 1945 with fellow directors William Wyler and Frank Capra (who described it as a "wonderful independent set-up that all the directors in the world were watching and hoping to emulate"), gave him "full autonomy" in his filmmaking, including "the right to edit, cut, and score" his work as he saw fit. The eventual failure of Liberty Films (the company was sold to Paramount over Stevens's objections after producing only one film, Capra's *It's a Wonderful Life*) was due in part to the three directors being ahead of their time. Though the company prefigured the independent movement in American cinema that exploded in the late 1960s, as Gene D. Phillips notes, in the 1940s "it was still a bit too early for Hollywood to accept fully the concept of independent production companies, since the studio system would remain in its heyday until the early 1950s."

In a well-publicized case, Stevens even sued Paramount and NBC in 1965 when the television network planned to screen *A Place in the Sun* in what he saw as "a distorted, truncated and segmented version." NBC, argued Stevens at the time, had replaced the film's dissolves with fades, and had inserted commercials "at the expense of the artistic integrity, the mood, effect, and continuity of the film . . . It's like taking the cadenza out of a concerto." His court case became something of a *cause célèbre*, and as the *New York Times* noted in May 1966, led a group of influential Hollywood directors "to launch a vigorous counterattack in their campaign to reduce or eliminate commercial interruptions from motion pictures shown on television."

"I have brought this action," explained Stevens (as quoted in *Variety*), "not only because of its significance as applied to the specific picture involved, but also because I think the issue is vital to all filmmakers and one of key importance to the general public. I believe that, with respect to a film which has been accorded the attention and acclaim of a vast audience, the film itself is entitled to receive, and the public to enjoy, the same integrity in its presentation which led to its original acceptance." In the same statement, issued at the time Stevens filed his complaint, he makes explicit reference to the "dollar and cents conjecture" that he discusses with Mary Ann Fisher in this volume. "A motion picture should be respected as being more than a tool for selling soap, toothpaste, deodorant, used cars, beer, and the whole gamut of products advertised on television," he told Fisher. "The audience too should be respected by being presented with a film as they remember it, and for those who have not seen it, as it was intended to be seen. Anything less is a degradation of the film and its audience."

Stevens commanded great respect from his fellow filmmakers, who elected him twice as president of the Screen Directors Guild. It speaks volumes that in the midst of problems during the filming of *The Greatest*

Story Ever Told, Jean Negulesco and David Lean (fresh from his international success *Lawrence of Arabia*) volunteered to assist by directing (uncredited) other camera units. Previously, in 1950, as McCarthyism swept through Hollywood, Cecil B. DeMille decided he wanted all members of the guild to sign a compulsory loyalty oath. When Joseph Mankiewicz, the guild's president, opposed such a move, DeMille sought to have him removed. On hearing of this battle, and wanting to distance himself as far as possible from DeMille, Stevens engaged a lawyer to investigate the situation, and then resigned from the guild's governing board. This move helped block what John Huston has described as a "putsch," and DeMille backed down. (The story goes that during their confrontation, implying he was doing nothing to stop the spread of communism in Hollywood, DeMille demanded to know where Stevens had been during the war. "I was up to my ass in mud at Bastogne, while you were fighting the battle of capital gains," replied Stevens.) Fred Zinnemann has said, "To the young members of the Directors Guild who were idealists and who wanted to make good films, George was a sort of Pope, or certainly a Cardinal. He was one of the few people who could stand up to the front office. We all learned that we could have some measure of success if we didn't give up. Nobody at the studios took film seriously as a creative medium. George was one of the people who instilled in the studios that film was more than that."

Though much of his filmography reads as a list of solid financial successes, Stevens was forever hoping to affect audience emotions rather than studio coffers. All of his films are emotionally honest, a reflection of Stevens's own way of looking at the world. In George Stevens Jr.'s film about his father, Stevens recalls walking through the gates of Dachau. "When a poor man, hungry and unseeing because his eyesight is failing, grabs me and starts begging, I feel the Nazi in myself. I abhor this man, and I want him to keep his hands off me. And the reason I want him to keep his hands off me is because I see myself capable of arrogance and brutality to keep him off me. That's a fierce thing, to discover within yourself that which you despise the most in others." And in terms of the industry he so loved, regardless of his box-office security at the studios for most of his working life, Stevens sought real change. The *Los Angeles Daily News* reported in 1948 that "Stevens would like to see the motion picture industry set up a fund for the production of non-commercial films, which could be turned out one a year by different studios, and exhibited in small houses. . . . It would offer an outlet for Hollywood's own craftsmen who deplore the emphasis on commercialization, and obviously it would please select audiences." (It was, in fact, George Stevens Jr. who founded such an organization in 1967: the American Film Institute.)

Today, Stevens's body of work seems more coherent and impressive when taken as a whole than if the films are looked at individually. Put together, the twenty-six features allow audiences to become better aware of the themes that so preoccupied the director throughout his career. Critic Gilbert Adair has written that at his most personal, "Stevens might be described as a chronicler of the *pursuit of happiness*, that craving for self-betterment." To Donald Richie, the key idea in Stevens's films—as seen in characters as diverse as Alice Adams, Anne Frank, Shane, Jesus, George Eastman in *A Place in the Sun*, and Jett Rink in *Giant*—is that of "how the outsider reacts to his situation." Something of an outsider himself, Stevens always had great respect for his audiences, who in turn responded positively to the profound humanism in his work, a quality that also shines through in this interview collection.

Though he sometimes spent months traveling the United States (and the world) on press tours to accompany his work, George Stevens did not give many in-depth interviews throughout his career. Fortunately, this volume benefits from several conversations never intended for publication. These pieces, under the attentive eye of George Stevens Jr., Stevens's son and a director in his own right, have undergone some editing in order to make them publishable, though in all cases an attempt has been made to retain Stevens's vernacular. The interview from the American Film Institute is not taken from the published version of the discussion held in May 1973, rather from the verbatim transcript held in the archives of the AFI library. Rather than naming those individuals in the audience who asked Stevens questions that day, all questions have been attributed to James Silke. The substantial interview with Robert Hughes was given in conjunction with the Museum of Modern Art's retrospective of Stevens's films in 1970 (which also resulted in Donald Richie's monograph *George Stevens: An American Romantic*). The text present here has been cut down from a verbatim transcript (marked "Never used") of approximately 250 pages. The title

"Getting the Belly Laugh" is my own. William Kirschner was an actor who appeared in *The Diary of Anne Frank*. His interview is drawn from the transcript of a conversation he did on behalf of the publication he was editor of, the *Jewish War Veterans Review*. Bruce Petri's contribution to this book is taken from the 300-page interview he conducted as research for his Ph.D. (see below), while the interview with Mary Ann Fisher is taken from the transcript of an interview Stevens gave to *Life* magazine in 1963 (the title of which, "A Dollar and Cents Conjecture," is also my own). The remaining pieces in this volume were selected from the surprisingly spare number of previously published interviews with Stevens located in archives stretching from Paris to Los Angeles.

The filmography below lists only those films Stevens worked on as director. For a comprehensive list of those shorts on which he was either cameraman or assistant cameraman, refer to Bruce Petri's thesis, published as *A Theory of American Film: The Films and Techniques of George Stevens*. (The AFI publication *Dialogue on Film* from 1973 also contains James Silke's useful filmography.) Richie's monograph and Ph.D. theses aside, there are no books about George Stevens's life and work, though there exist several interesting surveys of his films, most notably in Gene D. Phillips's *Major Film Directors of American and British Cinema* (1999). For discussions of *Shane*, readers are directed to two recent books: one by Edward Countryman and Evonne von Heussen-Countryman, published by the British Film Institute; the other by Michael F. Blake, entitled *Code of Honor: The Making of Three Great American Westerns* (Taylor Trade, 2003). George Stevens Jr. has also produced and directed two documentaries about his father's work: *George Stevens: A Filmmaker's Journey* (1985) and *George Stevens: D-Day to Berlin* (1994), which contains the color footage Stevens personally shot during the closing stages of the war in Europe, including what is probably the only color footage of the Normandy invasion of 1944.

Thanks to Peter Brunette, and Seetha Srinivasan, Anne Stascavage, and Walter Biggins at the University Press of Mississippi. Linda Mehr and Val Almenderez at the Margaret Herrick Library of the Academy of Motion Picture Arts and Sciences, home of the George Stevens Collection, gave invaluable assistance. Thanks also to Dottie McCarthy, and especially to George Stevens Jr., who has done so much to keep his father's legacy alive.

CHRONOLOGY

1904 Born in Oakland, California, on 18 December to Landers Stevens, a Pacific coast matinee idol and stage director, and Georgie Cooper Stevens, a well-known stage actress. Both were proprietors of a West Coast touring company. His maternal grandmother, Georgia Woodthorpe, was the toast of San Francisco during the Gold Rush days, and his uncle, Ashton Stevens, became a noted Chicago drama critic.

1909 Appears in a production of *Sappho* in San Francisco and later works as a child actor and stage manager at his parents' company. Earns money as a commercial photographer.

1921 The Stevens family move to Los Angeles where Landers works as an actor in Hollywood, Georgie as a bit-player, and George as an assistant cameraman.

1924 Joins Hal Roach Studios as an assistant cameraman, studying with Floyd Jackman, where he shoots many films.

1927 Cameraman on many Laurel and Hardy comedies, starting with *Slipping Wives*.

1930 Cameraman on Laurel and Hardy short *Another Fine Mess*.

1930 Writer and director on Roach's *Boy Friends* films. Marries Yvonne Shevlin in Los Angeles.

1932 Moves to Universal Studios and works as scriptwriter for producer Warren Doane. Stevens is soon directing shorts for Doane, starting with *The Finishing Touch* (1932). Son George Jr. born in Los Angeles.

1933 Directs his first feature at Universal, *The Cohens and Kellys in Trouble*. Moves to RKO studios where he works on "The Blondes and the Redheads" films, starting with *Flirting in the Park*.

1934 Directs his first drama, *Laddie*, with John Beal and Gloria Stuart.

1935 Katharine Hepburn asks Stevens to direct her in *Alice Adams*. Hepburn and the film receive Academy Award nominations. RKO releases *Annie Oakley* starring Barbara Stanwyck.

1936 The musical comedy *Swing Time* with Fred Astaire and Ginger Rogers.

1937 Directs *Quality Street* with Katharine Hepburn and *A Damsel in Distress* with Fred Astaire, George Burns, and Gracie Allen.

1938 *Vivacious Lady* with Ginger Rogers and James Stewart.

1939 Uncredited direction on *Having a Wonderful Time* with Ginger Rogers and Douglas Fairbanks Jr. Produces and directs the comedy adventure yarn *Gunga Din*.

1940 Melodrama *Vigil in the Night* with Carole Lombard.

1941 Becomes president of the Screen Director's Guild, a role he holds until 1943, and again from 1946 to 1948. *Penny Serenade* with Cary Grant and Irene Dunne, for which Grant receives his only Academy Award nomination. Moves to Columbia from RKO.

1942 Katharine Hepburn and Spencer Tracy's first pairing in *Woman of the Year* for which Hepburn received an Academy Award nomination. *The Talk of the Town*, starring Cary Grant, Ronald Colman, and Jean Arthur, is released, for which Stevens receives an Academy Award nomination as producer.

1943 Academy Award nominations as producer/director for romantic comedy *The More the Merrier*. Appointed head of the Signal Corps Special Motion Picture Unit and is assigned to photograph activities of all Allied military units in Europe. Stevens accompanies forces from Normandy through to Berlin, filming color 16mm footage of the liberation of Paris and the entry of Allied forces into Dachau.

1945 Released from military service with the rank of lieutenant colonel after winning five battle stars, the Legion of Merit, and a Unit Citation from General Eisenhower. Two films he worked on, *The Nazi Plan* and *Nazi Concentration Camps* are screened at the war crimes trials at Nuremberg. Establishes Liberty Films with directors William Wyler and Frank Capra, and producer Samuel Briskin.

1948 Directs *I Remember Mama* for RKO. Liberty Films is sold to Paramount Pictures. Directs a segment of *On Our Merry Way*.

1949 Divorces Yvonne Shevlin.

1950 Leads investigation by the Directors Guild of Cecil B. DeMille's effort to oust Joseph L. Mankiewicz as president.

1951 *A Place in the Sun*, starring Elizabeth Taylor and Montgomery Clift, wins five Academy Awards, including Best Director.

1952 *Something to Live For* with Ray Milland and Joan Fontaine.

1953 Directs and produces the classic Western *Shane* with Alan Ladd and Van Heflin. Wins Irving G. Thalberg Award.

1957 Wins Academy Award for Best Director and the Screen Directors Guild Award for his epic *Giant*, completed the previous year.

1958 President of the Academy of Motion Picture Arts and Sciences for a year. Wins D. W. Griffith Award for Lifetime Achievement from the Directors Guild.

1959 Releases *The Diary of Anne Frank*, based on Frances Goodrich and Albert Hackett's play, to great acclaim. Nominated for Academy Award for Best Director.

1960 Starts work on his biblical epic *The Greatest Story Ever Told* by researching in the Middle East.

1964 Appointed by President Lyndon Johnson to serve on newly created National Council on the Arts.

1965 Sues NBC and Paramount Pictures for screening a truncated version of *A Place in the Sun* on television. Judge rules in his favor that Paramount cannot cut the film, but in favor of NBC who can continue to insert commercials in films. *The Greatest Story Ever Told* is released.

1968 Marries Joan McTavish in Paris.

1970 Directs *The Only Game in Town* with Warren Beatty and Elizabeth Taylor.

1975 Dies in Los Angeles, 8 March.

FILMOGRAPHY

Shorts

1930
LADIES LAST
Producer: Hal Roach (Hal Roach Studios)
Director: **George Stevens**
Cast: Mickey Daniels, Grady Sutton, David Sharpe, Mary Kornman
20 minutes

1930
BLOOD AND THUNDER
Producer: Hal Roach (Hal Roach Studios, MGM)
Director: **George Stevens**
Screenplay: H. M. Walker
Editor: Richard Currier
Cast: Mickey Daniels, Grady Sutton, David Sharpe, Mary Kornman
18 minutes

1931
HIGH GEAR
Producer: Hal Roach (Hal Roach Studios, MGM)
Director: **George Stevens**
Screenplay: H. M. Walker
Cinematography: Ernest Depew
Editor: Richard Currier
Cast: Mickey Daniels, Grady Sutton, David Sharpe, Mary Kornman
22 minutes

1931
AIR TIGHT
Producer: Hal Roach (Hal Roach Studios)
Director: **George Stevens**
Screenplay: H. M. Walker
Editor: Richard Currier
Cast: Mickey Daniels, Grady Sutton, David Sharpe, Mary Kornman
17 minutes

1931
CALL A COP
Producer: Hal Roach (Hal Roach Studios)
Director: **George Stevens**
Screenplay: H. M. Walker
Editor: Richard Currier
Cast: Mickey Daniels, Grady Sutton, David Sharpe, Mary Kornman
20 minutes

1931
MAMA LOVES PAPA
Producer: Hal Roach (Hal Roach Studios, MGM)
Director: **George Stevens**
Screenplay: H. M. Walker
Editor: Richard Currier
Cast: Mickey Daniels, Grady Sutton, David Rollins, Mary Kornman
17 minutes

1931
THE KICKOFF
Producer: Hal Roach (Hal Roach Studios, MGM)
Director: **George Stevens**
Screenplay: H. M. Walker
Editor: Richard Currier
Cast: Mickey Daniels, Grady Sutton, David Rollins, Mary Kornman
21 minutes

1932
WHO, ME?

Producer: Warren Doane (Universal)
Director: **George Stevens**
Screenplay: Fred Guiol, James W. Horne
Cast: Mickey Daniels, Grady Sutton
20 minutes

1932
THE FINISHING TOUCH
Producer: Warren Doane (Universal)
Director: **George Stevens**
Screenplay: Fred Guiol, **George Stevens**
Cast: Richard Gallagher, June Clyde, Virginia Howell
20 minutes

1932
BOYS WILL BE BOYS
Producer: Warren Doane (Universal)
Director: **George Stevens**
Screenplay: Fred Guiol
20 minutes

1932
FAMILY TROUBLES
Producer: Warren Doane (Universal)
Director: **George Stevens**
Screenplay: **George Stevens**, James W. Horne
Cast: Richard Gallagher, June Clyde, Virginia Howell
29 minutes

1933
ROCK-A-BYE COWBOY
Producer: Warren Doane (Universal)
Director: **George Stevens**
Screenplay: **George Stevens**, James W. Horne
Cast: James Gleason (Jimmy), Marie Prevost (Marie), Vince Barnett (Slug), Raymond Hatton (Clem), Olive Cooper (Olive)
20 minutes

1933
SHOULD CROONERS MARRY
Producer: Warren Doane (Universal)
Director: **George Stevens**
Screenplay: James W. Horne, Fred Guiol
Cast: Jack Albertson, Greta Granstedt, Robert McWade, Johnny Arthur
21 minutes

1933
ROOM MATES
Producer: Warren Doane (Universal)
Director: **George Stevens**
Screenplay: Fred Guiol, James W. Horne
20 minutes

1933
QUIET, PLEASE!
Producer: Lou Brock (RKO)
Director: **George Stevens**
Screenplay: **George Stevens**, Fred Guiol
Editor: Tom Persons
Cast: Edgar Kennedy (Edgar), Florence Lake (Florence), Dot Farley (Mother), William Eugene (Brother)
20 minutes

1933
GRIN AND BEAR IT
Producer: Lou Brock (RKO)
Director: **George Stevens**
Screenplay: **George Stevens**, Fred Guiol
Editor: George Crone
Cast: Edgar Kennedy, Dot Farley, Fred Kelsey, Florence Lake
21 minutes

1933
WHAT FUR
Producer: Lou Brock (RKO)

Director: **George Stevens**
Screenplay: **George Stevens**, Fred Guiol
Editor: Edward Mann
Cast: Edgar Kennedy, Dot Farley, Fred Kelsey, Florence Lake
21 minutes

1933
FLIRTING IN THE PARK
Producer: Lou Brock (RKO)
Director: **George Stevens**
Screenplay: Fred Guiol, **George Stevens**
Cinematography: Len Powers, **George Stevens**
Editor: John Lockert
Cast: June Brewster, Charlie Hall, Edward J. Nugent, David Sharpe, Grady Sutton
20 minutes

1933
A DIVORCE COURTSHIP
Producer: Lou Brock (RKO)
Director: **George Stevens**
Screenplay: Jack Townley, Fred Guiol
Editor: John Lockert
Cast: Carol Trevis, June Brewster
21 minutes

1933
WALKING BACK HOME
Producer: Lou Brock (RKO)
Director: **George Stevens**
Screenplay: **George Stevens**, Fred Guiol
Editor: John Lockert
Cast: Carol Trevis, June Brewster, Landers Stevens
21 minutes

1934
OCEAN SWELLS

Producer: Lee Marcus (RKO)
Director: **George Stevens**
Screenplay: Fred Guiol, Jack Townley
Editor: John Lockert
21 minutes

1934
BRIDAL BAIT
Producer: Lou Brock (RKO)
Director: **George Stevens**
Screenplay: Jean Yarborough, Dick Smith
Editor: John Lockert
20 minutes

1934
ROUGH NECKING
Producer: Lou Brock (RKO)
Director: **George Stevens**
Screenplay: Fred Guiol, Jack Townley
Editor: John Lockert
21 minutes

1934
THE UNDIE-WORLD
Producer: Lou Brock (RKO)
Director: **George Stevens**
Screenplay: Jack Townley, Jean Yarborough
Editor: John Lockert
Cast: June Brewster, Guinn Williams, Grady Sutton
21 minutes

1934
CRACKED SHOTS
Producer: Lou Brock (RKO)
Director: **George Stevens**
Screenplay: Fred Guiol, Jack Townley
Editor: John Lockert
20 minutes

1934
STRICTLY FRESH YEGGS
Producer: Lou Brock (RKO)
Director: **George Stevens**
Screenplay: Fred Guiol, Jack Townley
Editor: John Lockert
21 minutes

1935
PICKLED PEPPERS
Producer: (RKO)
Director: **George Stevens**
Cast: June Brewster, Grady Sutton, Carol Tevis

1935
HUNGER PAINS
Producer: (RKO)
Director: **George Stevens**
Cast: Walter Brennan, June Brewster, Eddie Kane, Grady Sutton, Carol Tevis

Features

1933
THE COHENS AND KELLYS IN TROUBLE
Producer: Carl Laemmle Jr. (Universal)
Director: **George Stevens**
Screenplay: Albert Austin, Homer Croy, Fred Guiol, Jack Jungmeyer, Vernon Smith
Cinematography: Len Powers
Editor: Robert Carlisle
Cast: George Sidney (Nathan Cohen), Charles Murray (Patrick Kelly), Maureen O'Sullivan (Molly Kelly), Andy Devine (Andy Anderson), Jobyna Howland (Queenie Truelove), Maude Fulton (Miss Fern), Frank Albertson (Bob Graham), Henry Armetta (Captain Silva)
68 minutes

1934
KENTUCKY KERNELS
Producer: Lee S. Marcus, H. N. Swanson (RKO)
Director: **George Stevens**
Screenplay: Fred Guiol, Bert Kalmar, Harry Ruby
Cinematography: Edward Cronjager
Editor: James B. Morley
Cast: Bert Wheeler (Willie Doyle), Robert Woolsey (Elmer Dugan), Mary Carlisle (Gloria Wakefield), George McFarland (Spanky Milford), Noah Beery (Colonel Wakefield), Lucille La Verne (Aunt Hannah)
75 minutes

1934
BACHELOR BAIT
Producer: Pandro S. Berman, Lou Brock (RKO)
Director: **George Stevens**
Screenplay: Edward Halperin, Victor Halperin, Glenn Tryon
Cinematography: David Abel
Editor: James B. Morley
Cast: Stuart Erwin (Mr. William Watts), Rochelle Hudson (Cynthia Douglas), Pert Kelton (Allie Summers), Richard Gallagher (Bramwell Van Dusen), Berton Churchill (Barney Nolan), Grady Sutton (Don Belden), Clarence Wilson (Clement)
74 minutes

1935
LADDIE
Producer: Pandro S. Berman (RKO)
Director: **George Stevens**
Screenplay: Ray Harris, Dorothy Yost
Cinematography: Harold Wenstrom
Editor: James B. Morley
Cast: John Beal (Laddie Stanton), Gloria Stuart (Pamela Pryor), Virginia Weidler ("Little Sister" Stanton), Donald Crisp (Mr. Pryor), Dorothy Peterson (Mrs. Stanton), Willard Robertson (Mr. John Stanton), William Bakewell (Robert Pryor)
70 minutes

1935
THE NITWITS
Producer: Lee S. Marcus (RKO)
Director: **George Stevens**
Screenplay: Al Boasberg, Fred Guiol
Cinematography: Edward Cronjager
Editor: John Lockert
Cast: Bert Wheeler (Johnnie), Robert Woolsey (Newton), Fred Keating (William Darrell), Betty Grable (Mary Roberts), Evelyn Brent (Mrs. Alice Lake), Erik Rhodes (George Clark), Hale Hamilton (Lake)
81 minutes

1935
ALICE ADAMS
Producer: Pandro S. Berman (RKO)
Director: **George Stevens**
Screenplay: Dorothy Yost, Mortimer Offner, Jane Murfin
Cinematography: Robert De Grasse
Editor: Jane Loring
Cast: Katharine Hepburn (Alice Adams), Fred MacMurray (Arthur Russell), Fred Stone (Mr. Virgil Adams), Evelyn Venable (Mildred Palmer), Frank Albertson (Walter Adams), Ann Shoemaker (Mrs. Adams), Charley Grapewin (J. A. Lamb)
99 minutes

1935
ANNIE OAKLEY
Producer: Cliff Reid (RKO)
Director: **George Stevens**
Screenplay: Joseph A. Fields, Ewart Adamson, Joel Sayre, John Twist
Cinematography: J. Roy Hunt
Editor: Jack Hively
Cast: Barbara Stanwyck (Annie Oakley), Preston Foster (Toby Walker), Melvyn Douglas (Jeff Hogarth), Moroni Olsen (Colonel William Cody), Pert Kelton (Vera Delmar), Andy Clyde (James MacIvor), Chief Thunderbird (Sitting Bull), Margaret Armstrong (Mrs. Oakley), Delmar Watson (Wesley Oakley), Adeline Craig (Susan Oakley)
90 minutes

1936
SWING TIME
Producer: Pandro S. Berman (RKO)
Director: **George Stevens**
Screenplay: Howard Lindsay, Allan Scott
Cinematography: David Abel
Editor: Henry Berman
Cast: Fred Astaire (John Garnett), Ginger Rogers (Penelope Carroll), Victor Moore (Pop Everett), Helen Broderick (Mabel Anderson), Eric Blore (Gordon), Betty Furness (Margaret Watson), Georges Metaxa (Ricardo Romero)
103 minutes

1937
QUALITY STREET
Producer: Pandro S. Berman (RKO)
Director: **George Stevens**
Screenplay: Allan Scott, Mortimer Offner, Jack Townley
Cinematography: Robert De Grasse
Editor: Henry Berman
Cast: Katharine Hepburn (Phoebe Throssel), Franchot Tone (Dr. Valentine Brown), Eric Blore (Recruiting Sergeant), Fay Bainter (Susan Throssel), Cora Witherspoon (Patty), Estelle Winwood (Mary Willoughby)
83 minutes

1937
A DAMSEL IN DISTRESS
Producer: Pandro S. Berman (RKO)
Director: **George Stevens**
Screenplay: P. G. Wodehouse, Ernest Pagano, S. K. Lauren
Cinematography: Joseph H. August
Editor: Henry Berman
Cast: Fred Astaire (Jerry Halliday), George Burns (George Burns), Gracie Allen (Gracie Allen), Joan Fontaine (Lady Alyce Marshmorton), Reginald Gardiner (Keggs), Ray Noble (Reggie), Constance Collier (Lady Caroline),

Montagu Love (Lord John Marshmorton), Harry Watson (Albert), Jan Duggan (Mrs. Ruggles)
98 minutes

1938
VIVACIOUS LADY
Producer: **George Stevens**
Director: **George Stevens**
Screenplay: P. J. Wolfson, Ernest Pagano
Cinematography: Robert De Grasse
Editor: Henry Berman
Cast: Ginger Rogers (Francey), James Stewart (Peter), James Ellison (Keith), Beulah Bondi (Mrs. Morgan), Charles Coburn (Mr. Morgan), Frances Mercer (Helen), Phyllis Kennedy (Jenny), Grady Sutton (Culpepper), Alec Craig (Joseph)
90 minutes

1939
GUNGA DIN
Producer: **George Stevens** (RKO)
Director: **George Stevens**
Screenplay: Joel Sayre, Fred Guiol
Cinematography: Joseph H. August
Editor: Henry Berman, John Lockert
Cast: Cary Grant (Sergeant Archibald Cutter), Victor McLaglen (Sergeant MacChesney), Douglas Fairbanks Jr. (Sergeant Thomas Ballantine), Sam Jaffe (Gunga Din), Eduardo Ciannelli (Guru), Joan Fontaine (Emaline Stebbins), Montagu Love (Colonel Weed), Robert Coote (Bertie Higginbotham), Abner Biberman (Chota), Lumsden Hare (Major Mitchell)
117 minutes

1940
VIGIL IN THE NIGHT
Producer: **George Stevens** (RKO)
Director: **George Stevens**
Screenplay: Fred Guiol, P. J. Wolfson, Rowland Leigh
Cinematography: Robert De Grasse

Editor: Henry Berman
Cast: Carole Lombard (Anne Lee), Brian Aherne (Dr. Prescott), Anne Shirley (Lucy Lee), Julien Mitchell (Matthew Bowley), Robert Coote (Dr. Caley), Brenda Forbes (Nora), Rita Page (Glennie), Peter Cushing (Joe Shand)
96 minutes

1941
PENNY SERENADE
Producer: **George Stevens** (Columbia)
Director: **George Stevens**
Screenplay: Morrie Ryskind
Cinematography: Joseph Walker
Editor: Otto Meyer
Cast: Irene Dunne (Julie Gardiner Adams), Cary Grant (Roger Adams), Beulah Bondi (Miss Oliver), Edgar Buchanan (Applejack Carney), Ann Doran (Dotty), Eva Lee Kuney (Trina), Leonard Willey (Dr. Hartley), Wallis Clark (Judge), Walter Soderling (Billings)
119 minutes

1942
WOMAN OF THE YEAR
Producer: Joseph L. Mankiewicz (MGM)
Director: **George Stevens**
Screenplay: Ring Lardner Jr., Michael Kanin
Cinematography: Joseph Ruttenberg
Editor: Frank Sullivan
Cast: Spencer Tracy (Sam Craig), Katharine Hepburn (Tess Harding), Fay Bainter (Ellen Whitcomb), Reginald Owen (Clayton), Minor Watson (William Harding), William Bendix (Pinkie Peters), Gladys Blake (Flo Peters), Dan Tobin (Gerald), Roscoe Karns (Phil Whittaker), William Tannen (Ellis)
114 minutes

1942
THE TALK OF THE TOWN
Producer: **George Stevens** (Columbia)

Director: **George Stevens**
Screenplay: Irwin Shaw, Sidney Buchman
Cinematography: Ted Tetzlaff
Editor: Otto Meyer
Cast: Cary Grant (Leopold Dilg), Jean Arthur (Nora Shelley), Ronald Colman (Michael Lightcap), Edgar Buchanan (Sam Yates), Glenda Farrell (Regina Bush), Charles Dingle (Andrew Holmes), Emma Dunn (Mrs. Shelley), Rex Ingram (Tilney)
118 minutes

1943
THE MORE THE MERRIER
Producer: **George Stevens** (Columbia)
Director: **George Stevens**
Screenplay: Richard Flournoy, Lewis R. Foster, Frank Ross, Robert Russell
Cinematography: Ted Tetzlaff
Editor: Otto Meyer
Cast: Jean Arthur (Connie Milligan), Joel McCrea (Joe Carter), Charles Coburn (Benjamin Dingle), Richard Gaines (Charles J. Pendergast), Bruce Bennett (Evans), Frank Sully (Drunk), Clyde Fillmore (Senator Noonan), Stanley Clements (Morton Rodakiewicz)

1948
ON OUR MERRY WAY
Producer: Benedict Bogeaus, Burgess Meredith (Benedict Bogeaus, Miracle, UA)
Director: Leslie Fenton, King Vidor, **George Stevens**
Screenplay: Lou Breslow, Laurence Stallings
Cinematography: Gordon Avil, Joseph Biroc, Edward Cronjager, Ernest Laszlo, John F. Seitz
Editor: James Smith
Cast: Paulette Goddard (Martha Pease), James Stewart (Slim), Henry Fonda (Lank), Fred MacMurray (Al), Burgess Meredith (Oliver Pease), William Demarest (Floyd), Hugh Herbert (Eli Hobbs), Eduardo Ciannelli (Maxim)
107 minutes

1948
I REMEMBER MAMA
Producer: Harriet Parsons (RKO)
Director: **George Stevens**
Screenplay: DeWitt Bodeen
Cinematography: Nicholas Musuraca
Editor: Robert Swink
Cast: Irene Dunne (Mama), Barbara Bel Geddes (Katrin), Oskar Homolka (Uncle Chris), Philip Dorn (Papa), Cedric Hardwicke (Mr. Hyde), Edgar Bergen (Mr. Thorkelson), Rudy Vallee (Dr. Johnson), Barbara O'Neil (Jessie Brown), Florence Bates (Florence Dana Moorhead)
134 minutes

1951
A PLACE IN THE SUN
Producer: **George Stevens** (Paramount)
Director: **George Stevens**
Screenplay: Harry Brown, Michael Wilson
Cinematography: William C. Mellor
Editor: William Hornbeck
Cast: Montgomery Clift (George Eastman), Elizabeth Taylor (Angela Vickers), Shelley Winters (Alice Tripp), Anne Revere (Hannah Eastman), Keefe Brasselle (Earl Eastman), Fred Clark (Bellows), Raymond Burr (Frank Marlowe), Herbert Heyes (Charles Eastman), Shepperd Strudwick (Anthony Vickers), Frieda Inescort (Mrs. Vickers), Kathryn Givney (Louise Eastman)
122 minutes

1952
SOMETHING TO LIVE FOR
Producer: **George Stevens** (Paramount)
Director: **George Stevens**
Screenplay: Dwight Taylor
Cinematography: George Barnes
Editor: William Hornbeck
Cast: Ray Milland (Alan Miller), Joan Fontaine (Jenny Carey), Teresa Wright (Edna Miller), Richard Derr (Tony Collins), Douglas Dick (Baker), Herbert Heyes (Crawley), Harry Bellaver (Billy), Paul Valentine (Albert),

Frank Orth (Waiter), Robert Cornthwaite (Young Man), Helen Spring (Mrs. Crawley), Rudy Lee (Chris), Patric Mitchell (Johnny)
89 minutes

1953
SHANE
Producer: **George Stevens** (Paramount)
Director: **George Stevens**
Screenplay: A. B. Guthrie Jr. (additional dialogue by Jack Sher)
Cinematography: Loyal Griggs
Editor: William Hornbeck, Tom McAdoo
Cast: Alan Ladd (Shane), Jean Arthur (Marian Starrett), Van Heflin (Joe Starrett), Brandon De Wilde (Joey Starrett), Jack Palance (Jack Wilson), Ben Johnson (Chris Calloway), Edgar Buchanan (Fred Lewis), Emile Meyer (Rufus Ryker), Elisha Cook Jr. (Frank Torrey)
118 minutes

1956
GIANT
Producer: **George Stevens**, Henry Ginsberg (Warner Bros.)
Director: **George Stevens**
Screenplay: Fred Guiol, Ivan Moffat
Cinematography: William C. Mellor
Editor: William Hornbeck
Cast: Elizabeth Taylor (Leslie Lynnton Benedict), Rock Hudson (Bick Benedict), James Dean (Jett Rink), Carroll Baker (Luz Benedict II), Jane Withers (Vashti Snythe), Chill Wills (Uncle Bawley Benedict), Dennis Hopper (Jordan Benedict III), Sal Mineo (Angel Obregon II), Rod Taylor (Sir David Karfrey), Judith Evelyn (Mrs. Nancy Lynnton), Earl Holliman (Bob Dace), Robert Nichols (Pinky Snythe)
201 minutes

1959
THE DIARY OF ANNE FRANK
Producer: **George Stevens** (Twentieth Century Fox)
Director: **George Stevens**
Screenplay: Frances Goodrich, Albert Hackett
Cinematography: William C. Mellor
Editor: David Bretherton, William Mace, Robert Swink

Cast: Millie Perkins (Anne Frank), Joseph Schildkraut (Otto Frank), Shelley Winters (Mrs. Petronella Van Daan), Richard Beymer (Peter Van Daan), Gusti Huber (Mrs. Edith Frank), Lou Jacobi (Mr. Hans Van Daan), Diane Baker (Margot Frank), Douglas Spencer (Harry Kraler)
180 minutes

1965
THE GREATEST STORY EVER TOLD
Producer: **George Stevens** (UA)
Director: **George Stevens**
Screenplay: James Lee Barrett, **George Stevens**
Cinematography: Loyal Griggs, Willliam C. Mellor
Editors: Harold F. Kress, Art J. Nelson, Frank O'Neil
Cast: Max Von Sydow (Jesus), Michael Anderson Jr. (James the Younger), Carroll Baker (Veronica), Ina Balin (Martha of Bethany), Victor Buono (Sorak), Richard Conte (Barabbas), Joanna Dunham (Mary Magdalene), José Ferrer (Herod Antipas), Van Heflin (Bar Amand), Charlton Heston (John the Baptist), Martin Landau (Caiaphas), Angela Lansbury (Claudia), Janet Margolin (Mary of Bethany), David McCallum (Judas Iscariot), Roddy McDowall (Matthew), Dorothy McGuire (The Virgin Mary), Sal Mineo (Uriah), Nehemiah Persoff (Shemiah), Donald Pleasence (Satan), Sidney Poitier (Simon of Cyrene), Claude Rains (King Herod), Telly Savalas (Pontius Pilate), Joseph Schildkraut (Nicodemus), John Wayne (The Centurion), Shelley Winters (Woman of No Name), Ed Wynn (Old Aram)
199 minutes

1970
THE ONLY GAME IN TOWN
Producer: Fred Kohlmar (Twentieth Century Fox)
Director: **George Stevens**
Screenplay: Frank D. Gilroy
Cinematography: Henri Decaë
Editors: John W. Holmes, William Sands, Pat Shade
Cast: Elizabeth Taylor (Fran Walker), Warren Beatty (Joe Grady), Charles Braswell (Lockwood), Hank Henry (Tony), Olga Valéry (Hooker)
113 minutes

GEORGE STEVENS

INTERVIEWS

Flair for Make-Believe Runs in Line

WOOD SOANES / 1935

HOLLYWOOD MAY NOT BE GROWING UP, but its young folks are, and it is not uncommon today to find a familiar name attached to a new and youthful face in a position of considerable importance.

In one of his comparatively recent pictures, Cecil B. DeMille used a group of juniors, the sons and daughters of men and women whose names were and in some instances still are box office magnets. Von Stroheim, Chaney, Beery, even DeMille were represented in the lists.

So it was with almost a patriarchal air that I sat at tea one day and lunch the next with a youngster who was not so long ago little better than a babe in arms while his parents were distinguishing themselves as leading folk in the theater.

Here in Oakland today, a grandfather who is still in the prime of life can look back on the launching of one son as a drama critic to pass judgment on the histrionic abilities of another and younger boy, and who is now in a position to crow as the third generation steps into the limelight.

George Stevens and his brother Jack were children making nuisances of themselves at the Dewey, the Broadway, the Central and Ye Liberty Playhouse when Landers Stevens and Georgie Cooper were the toasts of the town. Today George Stevens is the toast of Radio, and his brother Jack, a crack camera man.

So Landers Stevens and I sat with J. Richard Ryan, once manager for the veteran dramatic stock king, while young George, just elevated to one of the ace positions in Radio's list of directors, tried to evade leading

From *Screen and Radio Weekly*, 21 August 1935.

questions and give off the impression that directing Katharine Hepburn in *Alice Adams* is just a job of work and not an Academy Award boon.

A cool young fellow, who is veteran in Hollywood despite his lack of years, young Stevens has climbed to the upper rungs of the ladder with so little fuss that his ascent has passed almost unnoticed. Not long ago he was a cameraman, then an assistant director, then involved in the production of comedy shorts.

Suddenly the tide turned. He went from comedy shorts, after a phenomenal series of hits, to full-length comedies, in the twinkling of an eye he was handed over the baton for the Wheeler and Woolsey features at Radio, and on the day he directed his final sequences of *The Nitwits*, he was assigned to the Hepburn picture.

I found him first in a shabby little office, to which access was available by passing only one secretary—positively a mark of Zorro—looking over some elaborate drawings showing the interior of a manse and splattered with dotted lines. The hen-scratchings attracted my attention and seemed to cry for explanation.

"Saves time," observed Stevens laconically after the introductions. "These are the camera set-ups. I get an idea of what I'm going to shoot here in the office, and we don't have to go in a huddle on the set every time we finish a sequence. Not only saves time, but saves tempers and keeps to schedule. That's an important item we're prone to overlook."

"The picture! Well, it'll be one of two things, and I wish I knew the answer. It will either be a great picture—but that depends on the luck I have in recapturing the Booth Tarkington spirit; or it will be just another movie—enhanced by the presence of Katharine Hepburn in the chief role. It looks as if it's up to me."

And that, in short, is Stevens's attitude. Most youngsters not long out of their teens would have been in a flutter. After all, it could be argued the strength of a story and a star depend on a director's career. Perhaps underneath the polo shirt, young Stevens's heart was racing a little, but if it were he's a better actor than his father.

"There's a lot of loose talk about new trends in entertainment tastes," he was saying a little later, "but that's twaddle. Every so often you hear that the public is tired of this or that, or wants this or that in the matter of pictures. As a matter of fact they go to the theater for the same reason today they went to the first show ever staged—to be entertained.

"They want to laugh a little, have their emotions jounced and live through romance. That's what they wanted back in the days of Ye Liberty. That's what they wanted when Booth was in his power. And that's what they wanted from Shakespeare and Burbage and, I venture to say, Euripides, Sophocles and even Thespis and his cart.

"In my opinion we don't need to worry about a new trend but rather about showmanship. We need human stories, consistently played and well-written, and presented by actors and actresses who have the ability to make fictional characters become realities. Stories about people everybody knows and understands always meet with popular response.

"The trick is to have them sincerely portrayed. They may vary in type and theme but if the human element is there, the public will like them."

The conversation turned to styles in acting and leading exponents of the art. Stevens was talking of the heartaches of a director in a position such as his when old-timers come in for jobs.

"It's hell I tell you," he said, showing emotion for the first time, "to sit here with one small part to fill and have the casting office send you half a dozen men to choose from, men whose names were once written in big letters in stage history and who are willing to work for peanuts today. It's worse for me, because so many of them know me.

"And it's hard to believe that some of them ever were at the top. If it weren't for the fact that my childhood memories are pretty keen and that Dad is able to recite the saga of their greatness, I'd doubt if some of them had ever stepped onto the stage. It's amazing how quickly you lose your grip when you lose your audience contact.

"You remember the days when they used to kid the actor with the loudest voice being the best actor. Well, what sense is there in shouting today, what point to facial expressions? The gallery is right in your lap. The last row in the theater hears as well, if not better than the first. Then, too, there's been a general cultural change.

"This new generation of actors and actresses have widened interests. They see more of life than their predecessors did.

"Take the thousands of fine actors who were in dramatic stock. They started as youngsters, sometimes fame didn't catch up with them, and they never left their original bailiwick. They rehearsed every morning and afternoon or did a matinee, they worked every night. After the show, they had an hour of recreation, and then started on next week's lines.

"What chance did they have to keep abreast of the times, to read the newest books, to see other plays, to make friends outside the profession? Very little. Today, stock is gone and the colleges are filling the novice ranks on stage and screen. The established players have frequent vacations on pay with opportunities for travel, and many paid lay-offs to improve their minds.

"Why I can remember when Dad used to get so jittery doing stock that he'd be forced to take a 'vacation.' And what would he do? Book himself and Mother on a vaudeville tour and off we'd go to see the country—doing two or three a day. It was great for Jack and me, but what did they get out of it beyond a change in environment?

"Take Miss Hepburn as a contrast. Her life is typical of most of the top flight. She practically commutes between New York and Hollywood, thanks to the swift transportation of today. She reads the best and newest books, available a few days before they're off the eastern presses. She sees the newest plays and attends the best concerts.

"When she is not working, she has the opportunity of getting away from the atmosphere of the screen and absorbing everyday life around her. She is able to keep a fresh viewpoint, and naturally that reflects itself in her work. Rubbing shoulders with men and women outside the profession makes it possible for her to depict them as she visualizes them.

"There's no reason for her to go stale. Hard work never hurt anyone, as the old proverb said. And that other old bromide about all work and no play is as true today as ever. If the theater isn't advancing today it certainly isn't because actors and actresses—and that goes for directors, too—aren't given unparalleled opportunities."

"That's true enough, son," chimed in the elder Stevens, Jack to his intimates and Landers to his public, "but I think you're feeling too sorry for us. We didn't have such a bad time of it. It's all comparative, after all, and if you insist on bromides, there's another: what you don't know won't hurt you.

"We may have seemed to work hard, but it was work we liked, and that's more than half the battle. We had as much fun playing on the stage as the audience did watching us. And there was a spirit of friendliness then that you youngsters haven't got, a spirit of camaraderie. If I blew up in my lines, it wasn't a tragedy, it was a laugh.

"You remember, Wood, the time we slipped one over on poor Henry Miller! He came out West all primed to show us boys what was what with his production of *The Only Way*. We found out that *The Only Way* was just another title for *A Tale of Two Cities*, so while Henry was billing for his $2.50 audiences, we splashed the town with *The Only Way* to see *A Tale of Two Cities* is to go to the Dewey.

"He was as mad as a hornet, but we both made money, and the audiences had a lot of laughs. We did it later, I remember, with *Hamlet*, and while I may not have been up on all of the nuances and symbols and interpretations, I gave very good account of myself in the role. Even your Uncle Ashton was so astounded he was speechless—he may have been drinking a little, but he was speechless.

"Seriously, though," the elder Stevens said turning to me, "I never had such an attack of stage fright as when I first worked for George. It was the darndest feeling. Since I've been living in Hollywood, I keep my hand in and pick up a pretty good salary playing bits, especially since real estate hit the toboggan.

"Well, sir, I walked on that set as kittenish as a novice, more so because I'd never been troubled with footlight fever. Every time I tried to say my few lines, I'd look at George sitting there as cool as a cucumber, trying to be helpful, think of the days when he was running around the stage, getting in my way, and I'd blow up higher than a kite.

"I don't know how I ever lived through the experience. Like stage fright, though, you get over it, and now I look forward to a small part in one of his productions. I like to watch him work. You know it's great to realize that you've not only raised two fine children, but that your neighbors—and audiences are always neighbors to me—appreciate them."

"Is my father talking about the glories of Glendale or the triumphs of my brother and me?" demanded George.

"He seems to be tooting his own horn in an oblique sort of way," I said.

"Then that settles it," George decided. "I'm paying this check, and the party's over."

Q and A

SCREEN AND RADIO WEEKLY/1939

"For the Colonel's Lady and Judy O'Grady
Are Sisters under their skins!"

GOOD OLD KIPLING!

He was chock-full of salty sayings about the facts of life. Ever since I was called upon to make a motion picture of *Gunga Din,* Kipling has been right at my elbow. He became more important to me than the assistant director, and I can assure you that no greater praise hath a director.

While the above quotation has nothing whatever to do with *Gunga Din,* it only goes to show what a wise old boy Kipling was. He knew most of the answers. For example, when a writer named Clarke Wales shot a rather embarrassing question at me, I simply yelled for Kipling instead of the assistant. We were hanging precariously on a parallel (camera scaffold) some forty feet in the desert air—Wales and I, not Kipling—and watching, from behind a motion picture camera, the thrilling charge of the British Lancers into an Indian ambush amidst the rocks of the prehistoric hills near Mount Whitney.

Wales suddenly nudged me, after the charge was over for the moment, and asked: "What qualifies a fellow like you, George, who has been making sophisticated comedies like *Vivacious Lady* and dance musicals like the Astaire-Rogers *Swing Time,* to direct this story of Indians and cowboys laid in India?"

He might as well have said "cops and robbers." I almost fell off the parallel. Then recalling his gift of asking embarrassing questions,

---

From *Screen and Radio Weekly,* 1939.

I retorted with Kipling's famous crack about the "Colonel's Lady and Judy O'Grady are sisters under their skins."

In sober retrospect of the query, which we have argued pro and con ever since, the Kipling crack still goes. They all look alike to me. Motion picture stories, I mean. Not wishing to take any bows for so-called versatility, I'll qualify by saying that it doesn't make any difference to me what sort of story I'm called upon to direct, if the story has something to say.

I look only for the basic idea. If in the situations the emotions are honest and the reactions natural, it doesn't make any difference to me whether the story is drama or comedy, slapstick or tragedy, musical or Western, cops and robbers or Indians and cowboys! The dialogue may be ultra in wit, the narrative may be fascinating writing—but if the story is only fancy dressing, I'll wait for the turkey. In other words, I won't worry about the dialogue until the time comes, and that time is when the actors are on the set ready to speak those certain lines.

If one considers the records of such outstanding directors as Frank Capra, Greg LaCava, Howard Hawks, and many others, versatility is the rule rather than the exception.

Between shots of the Lancers charging the Indians to the wild skirl of the Scottish bagpipes, we dangled in the air, swinging to and fro occasionally in the hot gusts of desert wind. As we gazed out over this strange sight on a desert waste of mountainous rocks and sands that have seen strange sights long before the memory of man, he asked: "Say, George, you were once a cameraman. Is that why you particularly wanted to film 'Gunga Din?' Do you always see a story photographically? Say for beautiful and awe-inspiring shots like this? Do you sort of read a story with a camera eye?"

My answer was "No!"

Maybe my old camera eye does register beautiful shots as I read, but if so I'm not conscious of it. No, not even when I read and reread "Gunga Din." While I am primarily a motion picture director, who firmly believes that the chief function of a picture is to move, I also firmly believe that a motion picture camera's place is right behind the lens.

Although once a cameraman, I duck all moving camera shots no matter how amazing and interesting they are to watch, because I feel that such photography distracts the audience, makes them conscious of the camera.

We, who were making a motion picture of Kipling's yarn for exactly 104 days, 75 of which were actually spent on location near Mount Whitney, had all sorts of embarrassing questions fired at us.

Why did the picture cost nearly $2,000,000?

Why did it take 104 days to shoot?

Why did we select a brilliant actor, but a middle-aged man like Sam Jaffe, instead of a youthful handsome lad like Uke Sabu to portray Gunga Din?

Why couldn't we have made most of the location scenes in process instead of going to the terrific expense of building an army cantonment, a Hindu village and a temple; and then establishing a company of hundreds of people for all that time, to make a picture?

All these questions came up, too, as we swung on our precarious perch up there.

In the first place, there would have been no sense in producing a picture of the Kipling classic unless it were made right. Also, if anyone reads "Gunga Din" carefully, they will immediately realize that here is a great idea for a motion picture. Is there a greater story in any language of the heroism of one of a downtrodden class of people?

"You limpin' lump o'brick-dust, Gunga Din!"

There is stark drama, pathos, and great beauty in that poem of a man.

We selected Sam Jaffe—remember his Grand Lama in Frank Capra's *Lost Horizon*?—because we wanted a man who could look like "you squidgy-nosed old idol, Gunga Din." We knew he could play the role to the hilt. Had we used a boy, we would have lost much of the dramatic power of the original story.

I can answer the questions about the cost of the picture, the length of filming time, and the use of actual locations, with no expense spared, in one sentence. Mechanical effects, no matter how marvelous, can never substitute satisfactorily for the real thing.

Speaking as a one-time cameraman who loves the wonders of a camera, the mechanical invention known in motion pictures as "process," which means photographing living actors against scenery projected on a screen, is remarkable in its effectiveness for a few scenes, but to attempt to photograph a great moving story by the trickery of mechanical effects would be as ridiculous as it would be unfair.

When Frank Capra wrote his recent article for this publication he commented on certain things that may be responsible for the depression at the picture theater box offices. Here is one he overlooked. In the old silent days, I recall the famous motion picture slogan that spelled Prosperity. It read something like this: "The movies take you everywhere."

Theater audiences miss the beautiful, breath-taking scenery we were accustomed to when silent pictures were made on location. Do you recall the vivid beauty of the old Bill Hart, Mary Pickford, and Doug Fairbanks pictures, for example? Those pictures made fortunes. Mostly, they were made on location. Or those beautiful Warner Bros. pictures of today, *Robin Hood* and *Valley of the Giants*?

To make *Gunga Din* in the studio would have been impossible and absurd; to make the picture on location meant that it would take twice as long to film and that it would cost at least twice as much as in the silent days. Why? Because sound recording requires much more painstaking care and time. Because everything has gone up, studio overhead, salaries, sound operation, equipment.

In *Gunga Din* we reverted to the good old silent days. The RKO-Radio studio took a terrific gamble, but we feel that it was worth it. I'll pay an honest tribute here to the two hundred hardy souls who labored uncomplainingly in a temperature of never less than 100 degrees, through June, July, and August; to them all—from the extras and studio workers to four swell guys named Gary Grant, Victor McLaglen, Douglas Fairbanks, Jr, and Sam Jaffe—for their sportsmanship on a tough job.

Yes, despite the seventy-five days in that broiling desert heat last summer, and the terrific strain on everybody concerned physically and mentally in making the picture under such trying conditions, it was worth the struggle.

But I did admit up on the parallel watching the endless charges of the Lancers across the desert wastes, that often when I crawled wearily into my camp cot at night, I muttered in my beard: "You're a better man than I am, Gunga Din!"

Making *Shane*

JOE HYAMS/1953

ONE DAY DIRECTOR GEORGE STEVENS looked out of the window of his study at home and saw four neighbor children playing "cowboys and Indians." They were dressed in the usual cowboy garb—broad-brimmed hats, colorful shirts and neckerchiefs—but what interested the director most was the way they "bang banged" indiscriminately at each other with their toy guns.

Finally one youngster jabbed a pistol in another's mid section and said, "Bang! bang! Fall down, you're dead." The "dead man" refused to fall, saying, "Who're you kidding? Guns don't hurt."

Mr. Stevens went away from his window thoughtfully. At the time he was working on the script of the new Western *Shane*, and the scene outside made a great impression on him. He knew where the youngster got the idea "guns don't hurt." It came from Western films which showed too much shooting merely for "orchestration purposes."

In recalling this story recently, Mr. Stevens said, "In most Westerns, everybody shoots and nobody gets hurt. One thing we tried to do in *Shane* was reorient the audience to the horror of a pistol. We used gunplay only as a last resort of extreme violence.

"There's no shooting in *Shane* except to define a gun shot, which for our purposes is a holocaust. It's not a gesture of bravado, it's death. When guns are used, they're deadly. Our characters have an abhorrence of violence and a knowledge of the responsibility of taking a life that doesn't exist in most Westerns."

"The principal terms of a Western are violence, but the results of violence are usually glossed over. In *Shane* a right-hand punch hurts. It can knock a man down, and a bullet destroys. When two men face each other with guns we go to great pains to point out that one is an upright figure of a man the moment before a trigger has been pulled. In the next moment he's a hunk of nothing in mind."

Mr. Stevens, who last year won both an Academy Award and the Screen Directors Guild Award for *A Place in the Sun*—the two highest film awards a director can get—told us he thinks *Shane* is his best film. New York theatergoers will have a chance to prove or disprove his contention next week when the picture is presented as the first film shown on a wide screen in the Radio City Music Hall.

A. B. Guthrie, a Louisville newspaper man and Pulitzer Prize—winning novelist for his Western, *The Big Sky* wrote the screenplay for *Shane*, with additional dialogue by Jack Sher. The film was based on an original short story by Jack Schaefer which appeared in *Esquire* magazine. When the story was first brought to Stevens's attention he decided he wanted to do it and Guthrie was the one man in the country to write the screenplay.

"I wanted Guthrie more than any other man to write *Shane* because I believed that he more than any one else was most familiar with the legend of the West," Mr. Stevens said. "I felt that after fifty years of motion pictures it was time for the Western legend to be redefined in its true terms or it would be lost.

"We attempted to be extremely authentic and accept the legend for what it possesses. We carefully reappraised it and put forth what we considered to be the embodiment of the Western legend, which is incidentally much the same legend as British knighthood, in which a single horseman rides to do battle against tremendous odds. Shane as played by Alan Ladd is the White Knight and Wilson, the hired killer played by Jack Palance, is the top of violence.

"Most present-day Westerns are inaccurate in even the smallest details. For example, there's no regard for clothing—the characters are dressed in garb just short of nylons and plastics. In casting we tried to get away from Sears Roebuck-type characters. Our women are frumpy and bedraggled-looking rather than glamorous, and our men wear beavers, not Stetsons."

One of the most memorable scenes in the film is built around a cemetery where a burial is taking place. The cemetery is on a hill in plain view of the town below. The scene has already come to be classed as a "Stevens touch."

"I got the idea for it from a small pioneer town of Bridgeport, California," the director said. "On a hill in back of the town there's a cemetery which was begun back in the early days because then death was a very large part of living.

"This relationship, which I consider important, was purposely established in the film by the cemetery scene in the hope that many in the audience would recognize it. The incident was in the picture because it brought to focus certain basic values such as life and death and it reintroduced the audience to the entire community and their problem."

"*Shane* is more than just a Western," Mr. Stevens believes. "It's an old-fashioned morality play aptly put together. We had a deep respect for the Western fable as such—that the good man always comes out on top; that right can have violence on its side; and that heroes can't have the comforts of ordinary men—but *Shane* is actually a passive story of a family and its benefactor.

"There's a present-day moral in *Shane* too. It takes great provocation to push people into the business of battle. But if they're pushed far enough they'd better get in and fight.

"In some sense Shane is a boy called to go into the Marine Corps because he's the strongest and best qualified to carry out his country's point of view. When you ask a man to fight and to take a life, you not only ask him to risk his own life but you ask him to make a great sacrifice of his moral ideals.

"All our sons, like Shane, are gunfighters, but no mother is breeding her son to be a gunfighter. Shane, the gunman, points up the sacrifices we call on our boys to make. He's a different man at the end of the picture, and we show this change in him through the character development of the boy Joe (played by Brandon De Wilde).

"The first time the boy sees Shane he's looking at him down the sights of a rifle barrel playfully aiming at him. When the film ends and Shane rides away saying, "There's no living with a killing, Joe," we believe that audiences will feel the boy has learned an important lesson about life."

George Stevens Puts Art, Business Together

HAL BOYLE/1953

TO SING A SONG, all you need is a voice. To paint a picture, all you need are brushes, colors, and canvas.

"But to produce and direct a movie today a man really ought to have two heads," says George Stevens, a man in a position to know.

"It is like trying to be a traffic cop and write a poem at the same time. You need an executive head to handle all the vast paraphernalia of movie-making. You need another, more sensitive head to get the delicate human emotional values you are trying to put on film."

Stevens, one of perhaps half a dozen authentic geniuses in his field in Hollywood, has a mind that combines both abilities. Each of his pictures bears the stamp of a man who knows people and takes infinite pains to portray them accurately. His latest, *Shane*, a story of the old gun-fighting west as seen through the eyes and heart of a small boy, raises the standard horse opera to the level of an art form.

"I try for reality," he said. "I like a story with enough drama in it so the actors don't have to steam themselves up and start behaving like actors instead of normal people."

George is a rugged, modest down-to-earth fellow himself who has managed to remain completely human in the unreal world of Hollywood.

"I have no truck with the social life there," he said. "I like baseball, and I like to hunt and fish. But the work of making movies is so varied itself it can give you all the pleasure and satisfaction you need."

From *Citizen-News*, 20 April 1953.

Stevens came from a prominent theater family himself. He started out as an actor, but overcome by a desire to eat regularly, he then became a cameraman, a gag writer, and a director of two-reel comedies.

"I suppose I made about thirty," he recalled. "In those days, however, we didn't count two-reelers—we accumulated them."

Since 1933 he had made twenty-one major films, including such hits at *Alice Adams, Quality Street, Vivacious Lady, Gunga Din, Woman of the Year, I Remember Mama, A Place in the Sun,* and *Something to Live For.* During the war Stevens directed forty-two armed-service cameramen in the filming of battle action in Tunisia and Europe, a monumental job for which he received no credit line—and wants none.

"After I came home, I wanted to do a really good film based on the Second World War," he said, and added wryly, "I thought that since I knew at least something of the local color of war, somebody would ask me to direct a war picture. I sat around waiting—and that was a big mistake. Nobody asked me. And now I am afraid it is too late."

But George is still yearning for the chance. He likes to vary his pictures.

"What kills off most directors," he observed, "is that they start repeating themselves—or begin taking themselves more seriously than they do their work. The biggest danger in Hollywood is to go Hollywood. You can't just make new pictures based on previous pictures that did well. You have to keep in touch with real people and real events."

George likes to keep things simple. It still amazes him that it requires scores or hundreds of technicians to film a single scene.

"You have a Grand Central Station atmosphere around you," he said, "and in all that wilderness of people and machinery perhaps the only thing you are trying to record is a small boy, crying goodbye. With all that organization you feel you ought to be filming a battlefield. You have to squeeze so much grapefruit—to get so little juice."

Diary of Anne Frank on Movie Set

FRED HIFT / 1959

ON STAGE 14 AT TWENTIETH CENTURY FOX the lights have recently dimmed on one of the most interesting and ingenious film sets to be built in many a year. It is the three-story house which George Stevens used to shoot *Diary of Anne Frank*, and it is, of course, an exact copy of the actual building and the "secret annex" in which young Anne and seven others spent two anxious years hiding from the Nazis.

For the stage play on which this movie is based, Boris Aronson created an imaginative set, which allowed continuous action. In the film all parts of the house, from the spice factory on the ground floor up to the tiny attic room, have been built into one huge set.

"We had a good many discussions on how to handle this problem of the hiding place," Mr. Stevens said. "When the Hacketts (Albert Hackett and Frances Goodrich) submitted their first draft of the screenplay, I was surprised to see that they had taken the camera out of the building. They felt, and perhaps with some merit, that the movie had to have wider scope. In fact, the original idea was to expand the whole story beyond the time covered by the play."

We were sitting in the director's spacious office on the Twentieth Century Fox lot. In a corner stood a scale model of the house in Amsterdam, each detail minutely reproduced. Mr. Stevens got up and walked over to it. His finger toyed with the tiny bookshelf which concealed the entrance to the Franks' hide-out.

"In the end, we decided to stay in the house," he said. "A lot of the artfulness of the play was in the skill with which it conveyed the cellular confinement of this little group of people. What we have done is to put the hiding place into an area where it is surrounded by other sets.

"Anne was thirteen when the family went into hiding. For two years, she could not set foot outside this place. To her, the outside world consisted of what she could hear from the room next door and the room below. The awareness of these people was primarily in what went on around them in the building. That is why some of the romantic passages in Anne's diary are so remarkable. This was a terrible experience, being crowded into such a small space with a lot of adults, and yet she remained cheerful and smiling, and she never gave up hope."

In the movie Anne Frank is played by newcomer Millie Perkins. Her parents are portrayed by Joseph Schildkraut and Gusti Huber, who had the same parts in the play. Shelley Winters, Lou Jacobi, Ed Wynn, Dick Beymer, and Diane Baker round out the small cast.

Their real-life counterparts went into hiding during the summer of 1942. The Gestapo finally caught up with them on August 4, 1944, and they all went to concentration camps. Only Otto Frank, the father of Anne, returned after the war. Christians, who had risked their lives to hide the Franks, gave him the diary which they had picked up off the floor in the annex after the Gestapo raid.

It should have been a grim play, but it wasn't. And the movie will not dwell on the depressing aspects of the story either. "Our emphasis is on that wonderful little girl who was Anne," Mr. Stevens stressed. "She had an inner light, a warmth that not even the terrible experience of confinement could douse. When you read the diary, it is full of hope and eagerness. Anne was tested, and in her trial she turned to the enduring things and away from bitterness. Anne faced life with her enchanting young spirit, and I think that is why her diary has moved so many young people who have written beautiful letters to Otto Frank."

George Davis did the original set design, and then Mr. Stevens called in Mr. Aronson as a consultant. "I wanted an almost poetic atmosphere around the hide-out rooms. Anne was young and romantic. In the film, when the Gestapo arrive, she is sitting at the window in the attic, looking out over a narrow street where white linen floats from wash-lines in a gentle breeze. To her, this had to make up for the wonders of nature of which she was deprived," the director said.

Mr. Aronson, who was busy on a play, took a plane to Hollywood and during the trip he sketched some ideas on the back of an old envelope. They were integrated into the set which was then rising on stage 14.

Mr. Stevens insisted on complete realism. The attic was lit by a single bulb hanging on a cord from the ceiling. "It was a difficult set to light," he recalled. "We increased the wattage of the bulb, and it gave us enough light to shoot, but at the same time it tended to glare. We got around that by painting out the side of the bulb that faced the camera."

Rehearsals took place on the set, in rooms surrounded by four walls. When it came to shooting a scene, Mr. Stevens had one of the walls removed. The whole huge structure stood on springs. In the scenes when the building is shaken by falling bombs from Allied planes, it was the set that took the beating. Normally, such effects are simulated by moving the camera. During breaks in the work schedule, Mr. Stevens had classical music played over the loudspeaker system to keep his actors "in the mood."

Otto Frank, who has never seen a performance of *Diary of Anne Frank*, saw the set when he visited Hollywood. Some months before that, he had shown Mr. Stevens over the actual house in Amsterdam. When he entered the hide-out room on the set, he stopped and his eyes clouded. He walked over to the window and stood there a long time, silent. Then he turned to Mr. Stevens and, with a sad smile, said: "How ironic it is, George. Here we are on a movie set, in a room that Anne called her home. There will be a whole film made about her. And yet, the one dream she had was to come to Hollywood and be a movie star."

Conversation with George Stevens

WILLIAM KIRSCHNER/1963

WILLIAM KIRSCHNER: *I'd like to talk about your experience of being at the camp in Dachau during liberation.*

GEORGE STEVENS: I got a signal back from divisional headquarters that I should get everyone available to me in my unit down to Munich. We had sound recording cameras, the only ones in existence at the time. The 69th Infantry Division was the one that liberated Dachau, and it was coming up from the south, and so we had to get down there. We loaded up our jeeps with weapons—we had a .50-caliber in each jeep, and a tommy gun, and some of those little German machine guns. We had a guy standing on the back with the .50-caliber, and we just took off across country. We'd stop off the road when we were going to eat our K-rations and all that. We ran into Patton's tanks on the autobahn. Christ, he ran tanks so damn fast! When we got down south into Bavaria, before we got to Nuremberg, we turned around a field, passed a barn, and there was a whole German infantry company sitting there, with their suspenders down and their coats off, and their weapons laying around. And Jesus, they look at this little group of jeeps coming along, you know, with all this stuff hanging out the side, and they look at us, and they turn away, and they mind their own business. Well, we got down to Dachau that evening. We were all billeted in a house, and a couple of guys, the combat photographers that had come up with the other outfit, had joined us.

It was unbelievable. What is there to say about such enormities and misfortune and abuse. A fellow in my unit who was something of a

From the *Jewish War Veterans Review*, August 1963.

linguist wrote letters for the dying to their relatives without interruption for days and nights at a time. It was like wandering around in one of Dante's infernal visions. A poor man, hungered and unseeing because his eyesight is failing, grabs me and starts begging. I went into a room in one of the buildings where they were interrogating SS soldiers. They had this old man—I say old, but I wouldn't say old today—on his knees, and behind him is a GI with a rifle butt, and the man is screaming. A Polish camp prisoner had caught him up the road on a farm wagon heading for Munich and brought him back. The strange thing is that at the end of the room were SS officers and soldiers stripped to the waist. I never saw such a ridiculous operation, waiting their turn for this, after which they were sent down to be rehabilitated. That night I was with Ivan Moffat who speaks good German, and we went over to these fellows who were laid out, and this old man says, "Americans are supposed to be honorable people. They're dirty torturers."

WK: *Could you tell me about your recent visit to Dachau?*

GS: I went to Munich and rented a car because I didn't want to be escorted, and pursued my recollection of the war. I wanted to see if I could find my way to Dachau, and though I did have a little difficulty—things have blossomed down there since the war—something helped me find it. I was completely transported back to the last time I had been there. The locals today are proud of their town. It's changed considerably and is a real community today. There used to be a main street that ran across what they called SS Strasse. Down the street was the post office and a supply store, a little pub and some two-story green buildings that were the billets for the SS officers. When we arrived during the war we moved into one of them on the corner where we could look into the main yard of the camp.

Fifteen years later, here was Dachau without—to me at least—any significance. A disappointment perhaps, because the least one could hope for from a great wrong is to be shown the way of that wrong. The greater the wrong, the more lasting the memory. But here was the greatest of wrongs simply swept away, here on this site without recollection. What surprised me was that I drove into the camp past a GI guard—the place was an installation for some American troops—and I see in front of me, on a building, the Nazi eagle. It looked exactly as it did the day we left it. I was with my son George, and we took a picture of it. I couldn't imagine why this symbol, designed by Hitler's people, was still there. The Americans there, rather than converting it to the new democracy, just ignored it, or had no consciousness of what it stood for.

So I try to get my bearings now that I'm inside this place. Before I left California I had put four or five photographs in a small postcard size tin box. I had taken them back in 1945. I wanted to have them with me and relate what I was looking at to these photos. While I was walking through, there was an American sergeant taking a girl through. He's talking like hell, "Yes, these were the crematoriums. I don't really know what happened in this room." I said, "Sergeant, I'll show you what it was," and I reached into my pocket and showed him these pictures of the bodies piled up. He looked at them like I'm crazy, and looks at the girl, and just walks away as if he's just met a mad man.

I wanted to go back to Bergen-Belsen too and got a car up at Hamburg. I didn't know the way and didn't have a map, so I got the car and went to a gas station where there was an English-speaking guy, and he had a big map on the wall. I asked him where Bergen-Belsen was, and he looked at me and says, "What's that?" I said, "Where they used to have the big concentration camp." "I never heard of it," he says. So I look at this map, and see that Bergen-Belsen is not on the highway map. I knew roughly where it is, so I started driving down. Here I am in Hamburg, and before you get to Hanover there's a turn-off. It's a beautiful day, I've got a nice Mercedes, sailing along through this green German countryside with all the little buildings made of red brick, and finally I come to a town called Belsen. No Bergen, just Belsen. That's what fooled me—the little town's name was Belsen. I drive down this little road for quite a way and come to a barracks, an old German troop barracks, and there are British soldiers there. I ask the sentry, "Where is Belsen, the old concentration camp?" And he says, "It's down the road about a mile or so, straight ahead."

So I go on down there, and sure enough there's the stone gate, and everything else as far as you can see is gone. I park the car and start walking, and guess I cover a couple of miles all over the place trying to figure it out. There is higher ground with some blocks that had burned down, some little memorial stones that people have put there in respect for people who died there, and a series of graves. I was curious about the area where Anne Frank had been, and also another area where there had been just acres of open country before they put the prisoners in blocks, and where they had put up tents. I walked all over the place trying to get it all straight in my mind, the actuality of what had gone on there, because it's something that the mind tends to throw off.

When we were at Dachau I went into that room where they had been interrogating these men and saw something I hadn't noticed at the time. There was a little window from where they could watch the gassing. Nothing has ever disturbed me in my life as much as the Hitler outrages. It's the reason I got in the war, and I finally wound up in a concentration camp on the day it was liberated. I hated the German army. What they stood for was the worst possible thing that's happened in centuries.

WK: *The wartime experience seemed to give some Hollywood directors a different outlook on life. Do you think that happened in your case?*
GS: I'm sure it would happen to anyone who had similar experiences to my own. The war gave us all a lot of time for thinking, to see people at their very best and their very worst. People with strength and people with utter weakness. It was an elaborate change in my life. I'm only aware of it because of how it changed my professional instincts. Otherwise I probably would not have analyzed myself so much. Professionally, I knew I wanted to do very different things to what I'd done before. In this respect, the film that was very important to me was *The Diary of Anne Frank.*

One important aspect of the war was getting away from the bench, of moving into another activity. I made film comedies, and after three years or more of war I came back and tried to make another comedy, and I couldn't do it. I started work on one with Ingrid Bergman, who was the number one star in America at that time. At one point she said, "Where's our comedy?" And finally I said, "This just isn't going to be funny, so we better forget it."

WK: *I was very impressed with the amount of research you did when you made* The Diary of Anne Frank. *It all felt so real.*
GS: There was an enormous amount of reality and authenticity in that picture. I felt we had to be tremendously exact because we were

dealing with a genuine piece of writing and it wasn't our business to change anything. Tony Van Renterghem, who was our technical advisor on the film, was in the underground in Amsterdam during the war and had elaborate and useful observations in many areas. We made detailed pictures of the actual rooms in the house and built sets in Hollywood. But I made drifting shots from the canals in Amsterdam to the front of the house into the interior of the house.

Before I did the picture I went to Amsterdam to visit Otto Frank, Anne's father. I would sit up in the attic with Otto for an hour at a time. It was the first time he'd been back there since the day they were all taken away by the police. It was like opening a grave, sitting and talking with this man. Tears would come to his eyes at the slightest recollection. One morning we were sitting there and there was a bird under the roof. The wings flapped and it flew out of the window, and Otto was so shocked that there was life in this building. I think he thought something had returned. The house is now a museum. I am told that most of the visitors come from America. At the time I was researching the film, I was told that there were lots of young visitors from Germany who sort of came to do penance. They felt some responsibility because they were the children of the people who had brought this about.

I've always been of the opinion that a director should never touch a film without his having a basic knowledge of its contents. Whenever we hit a stumbling block in translating from the stage to the film medium, not only did I return to the original diary for help, but I also returned again to the concentration camp areas and roamed houses in Amsterdam in the quarter where Anne lived where I talked with countless people who had survived the Nazi period there.

In *The Diary of Anne Frank*, we tried to depict the happenings mainly through Anne's eyes. I might say through the eyes of a child of the world, a child who had the ability to lead a rich and hope-filled life, a child who was inwardly indestructible and even in the most difficult situations did not lose her faith in the essential good of man. A child who could even repeatedly smile in the face of adversity. Naturally, Anne Frank's story is much greater and far-reaching than the movie which has its own technical and temporal limitations. Anne's existence is actually a story in several sections: a story which begins in Frankfurt-am-Main where she lived with her family. Then comes the emigration to Holland, the invasion there of the Hitler hordes, the forced uprooting of the Jews, the years in hiding and finally the tragic end. What we have filmed is the story of Anne Frank in hiding, the Anne Frank who knew nothing of the concentration camps as we now do.

I wanted to make a film about a human being who knew how to conduct herself in a time of overwhelming misfortune, even though the audience knows from the outset what Anne doesn't know: her ultimate fate. Thus one sees the life of a family, an average family, but one that is lacking one thing: freedom. And a family which is invisibly surrounded by an enemy which would deny it the right to breathe. By having written down her experiences, Anne mystically discovered the secret of how to make mankind think.

WK: *The motion picture industry has been sick of late. Do you think it will ever get well?*

GS: I have certainly lost no confidence in the medium of film as a communicative force. The business of people gathered together in great numbers to look at a screen and agree or disagree upon ideas as acted out in front of them, I think it's one of the great adventures of our time. I don't think any form of management or mismanagement is going to alter that. It's a force that's there for people to use and to engage in. I think the fellow who said that the motion picture is in its infancy said it too soon. He should wait another twenty years and then repeat it, because I think people are just beginning to discover the full value of the motion picture.

A Dollar and Cents Conjecture

MARY ANN FISHER/1963

MARY ANN FISHER: *What makes a great film director?*
GEORGE STEVENS: It has to do with the ability to have made films that are extremely worthwhile, and also having had the good fortune to have them be seen. I should think that awareness of the behavior of people is also important—how they talk, act, react. Remember that the camera is not the instrument. People are always the instrument. I love going to see films where I can learn about people.

MAF: *What is your method or approach?*
GS: Well, if you're relating me to the first question, that certainly puts me at a disadvantage because I make no presumption of being a great director. I think the misfortune of many people who conscientiously set about to direct films is that they can be discouraged by thinking too much about their status in relation to other filmmakers.

My approach to making a film? That's a big question—have we got a lot of tape on that machine? I wouldn't know how to define a specific approach to making a film. I suppose it would have to do with the subject matter. The variety of subject matters would all have to be dealt with differently. It's essentially reduced to stages: the planning when the script is devised and completed, the business of filming, then the all-important aspect of putting the film together in a form that is pleasant.

MAF: *To what extent is it necessary for you to take part in writing the script?*
GS: For me it's absolutely necessary to start from the very beginning. I can't think of coming and contributing something anywhere along the line other than the very start.

Interview conducted in September 1963; transcript from the archives of George Stevens.

MAF: *In working with the film from beginning to end, what is the role of the producer?*

GS: You have these terms, the producer-director, the writer, and so forth. I think the variety of usages of those particular aspects of film production vary so greatly that definition in one area wouldn't be quite the same definition in another area. I personally like to see films that are the work of as singular a consciousness as possible. By that I mean of one individual, not a group around a table.

MAF: *You edit your own films. How do you cut them?*

GS: I think there's no more important service to a film than the editing. The cutter is tremendously important on a film. As I have always worked with a very good editor, the best man I can get, or sometimes on a picture where there's a lot of film, two or three people. But the actual syntax of the picture—the arrangement of shots and the style, the flow—these things are purely arbitrary and often, if well done, the audience does not even notice them. This is all to do with the business of the film's architecture, building particular scenes and then laying those pieces in to suit that scheme.

I learned an interesting thing about cutting when I was watching Fred Astaire and Ginger Rogers on screen. I would cut the dance sequences, and when I did this found that the build-up was never quite as good. All of the mounting enthusiasm, this discovering of extraordinary magic one with the other, created a fine cinematic experience for the audience. The longer they danced together without a cut, the more involved the viewer became in what they were doing. If they could go through this whole elaborate, intricate routine, with the music building, then a *diminuendo* and *crescendo*, and they keep their steps together, by the time they danced off and the stage was left bare, there had been such an accumulation. If there had been a cut, it would have been lessened.

Actually, I hate the word "cutting," and the word "editing," because it's really "composing"—composing the relationship of images, and it has a variety of laws that must be met or else it's illiterate. You'll notice the joy some people have in seeing a work of the novice filmmaker, often an intellectual mind, where the camera is moving and always making itself known. I note that the critics seem to find this very expressive.

But to me it is as expressive as a man stumbling around to find the keys of the piano when he is trying to play a sonata.

MAF: *I was told you cut in the projection room, rather than directly on an editing machine.*
GS: Yes. The movieola is a picture hardly bigger than a postage stamp. Our responses to images have a great deal to do with how large they are, and I think the business of cutting and editing and balancing a picture on a tiny little screen like that distorts the effect. One has to make quite a transition in your mind to establish what that picture would look like when projected onto a large theater screen.

MAF: *How do you work with actors? You have always managed to get wonderful performances in your films.*
GS: There are so many aspects to the relationship between the director and the actor. I am inclined to say that it is a relationship of confidence. Mutual respect is important, and confidence is also necessary on the actor's part. A director should always be aware of the extraordinary discomfiture an actor must bear when up there in front of the lights, exhibiting himself or herself. My primary interest, I think, apart from achieving the required result of the scene, has to do with seeing to it that the actor is as comfortable as possible, though of course some people have to be somewhat disturbed to do a certain kind of work.

To an actor who is totally equipped to do everything in the way of acting, it can be helpful to give a little suggestion or some guidance here and there. That kind of actor will turn to the director as a response to what he is doing. Then there are other actors, like Rin Tin Tin, who really need a director entirely, by one means or another, to produce activity on the screen. I have worked on pictures in which I have had very little to do with the actors and actresses because they happen to be very well qualified. In the most practical way, if an actor doesn't need help, don't disturb his assurance in any way. If an actor needs not only help, but strength too, give them all of that. Give them something to stand up with, and if they are still lost, give them a concept of the role and the reading of the line. And always do it quietly, not with the other actors around. I think that an actor has the right to call on a director, whenever it is necessary, and particularly if the director is responsible for the story, which is often the case. It's possible to have a script where it is not entirely clear what the aim of the story is. There might also be humor intended that is not explicit in the script.

I feel that my real job as a director is just to be a kind of host on the film set. I have to be able to explain to the actors everything they need to know about the characters they are playing, to create backgrounds for each person depicted in the story we are telling. I have to help create very tangible and convincing people on the screen, and blend that with the actors' own interpretations of their roles so the story is as convincing as possible.

MAF: *To what extent do you allow the actor to interpret the role?*

GS: I think a good presumption is to allow the actor to interpret the role entirely, from beginning to end. I know some actors continually ask, "What about this? What do you want me to do? How should I do this?" But I like to see scenes played with as little conversation between as possible. There is always an understanding about the role and the story before we start filming, and I don't like to bring these ideas out just before they are about to play a scene. I want them to go out there and express themselves, do it the way it feels to them. If they are in trouble, of course they are grateful for any assistance you can bring them. Most often, if the actor understands the nature of the scene, I don't need to say anything.

MAF: *What do you think of actors?*

GS: That's like asking, "What do you think of people?" The first thing I remember in life are actors. My father was an actor, my mother was an actress. To me, actors are people, though don't ask me what kind of people.

MAF: *What do you feel has been your most successful film?*

GS: I have made it a point never to appraise anything that I do. I am always curious about what the response to a film might be, and it's very easy to get an appraisal on a work that's widely exhibited, so that spares me the responsibility of making judgments on my films. One thing that interests me is how short-lived most films are. I've always been interested in a particular film based on the presumption of how it might be received by an audience. I remember back when I started making films, I was curious to make a film that I wanted to do and that would be acceptable at that time, but might also be accepted five, ten, twenty years from now. From time to time there comes a film that I made a speculation about, and have now, over a span of years, seen reactions to it change tremendously. I think for a film to be of considerable merit means that it should be accepted by audiences over a long period of time.

As far as the favorites of my own films, I have a warm spot in my heart for *Shane*. It was enormously satisfactory to me from many standpoints. It was exciting work to do amidst the beautiful landscapes of Wyoming. We were attempting something on more than one level, more than just the surface level. That's where a film gets most interesting to me, with those aspects of it that are somewhat hidden, the secondary and third levels of interest. I've always wanted to keep audiences excited and interested at the same time as these secondary currents run across the screen and affect their conscious response.

MAF: *What do you think of the so-called "auteur" theory of filmmaking?*
GS: Those are the kinds of films I like to see—as singular as you can make the point of view. Only then does a film take on definition for me. The "auteur" concept is certainly the most desirable form of filmmaking, from my point of view.

MAF: *Do you think that recent European films—for example the work of Fellini or Resnais—have influenced American films?*
GS: Not much. I don't think they've had enough influence on American films. These European directors—and I know a number of them—are making films principally to make films. If they become secure financially along the way, that's fine. But I know in most of these instances, these directors would pay to make a film rather than necessarily be paid for it. That motivation gets a very sincere response from audiences. I think the audience is aware of it, I think they know they're seeing something that is made for them and for their minds to respond to. These kinds of films are not made just to lure audiences in.

But things are different here in our scheme of things, and it's high time American audiences, as well as American filmmakers, wake up to this idea that they shouldn't be confining their films to past practices. We need to realize that there are new ways of making films, and that the patterns we've been working with are not the patterns of tomorrow. What they should be doing is looking into the future and the continuing possibility for the development of the film into its ultimate means of expression. I don't think that it's the filmmakers who necessarily need to change, nor the exhibitors. It's the American audiences who regard films entirely differently than people in Italy, France, and even England. In most countries other than America, audiences take their motion pictures very seriously. They're stimulated by them, moved by them. Perhaps they get other rewards from them. But we've put a demand on our audiences that says a film should be quite a simple matter, something to be forgotten the second they hit the sidewalk. Audiences have always tried to work against this, but there isn't the kind of writing about cinema in America that you find in France or Italy or England. We like movies, and they like films over there. We have lots of movies and TV over here, but we also need good cinema.

MAF: *What do you feel are the problems the American film industry is suffering from?*

GS: I think one of the real misfortunes with our American motion picture has to do with the fact that it is almost entirely a dollar and cents conjecture. Everyone is interested in the commerce of it. I think there is much more to it than commerce. I think the ideas we are able to express in film are of untold worth, something much more acknowledged in other countries. But I do think this situation has improved tremendously from the days of the monolithic big companies, because American audiences are becoming more interested and more vocal about what they come upon in motion picture theaters. There have certainly been developments in recent years that give great promise for the future.

The industry here is making films not from life, but from other films. The producers think they are making pictures, but it's really just a production line turning out films that have been done before. All the components will come from other pictures, and too many of them will turn out last year's model for you. I've been watching this over a long period of time. The films that are made solely for the purpose of making money do not do well. Film is an extraordinarily persuasive medium, and if there is not something in the film that is there because a writer or director wants to make that particular film and tell that particular story, it will most likely not be a success. Of course, this gives those individual filmmakers who want to make films for some reason other than money to excel in their work. If a film sets out on a formula only to make money, the producers will find themselves in the situation of some of our big companies today that run their business from a high-level management area, and where it's not actually the filmmakers who make the films.

Stevens Talks about Movies

JAMES SILKE / 1964

STEVENS IN CONVERSATION is like Stevens making a film. As ideas, thoughts, or moods strike him, he will pursue them to draw as much from each as possible. Often he will pause at length and silently review a question or a statement in his mind, making sure that he takes everything into account before responding. His enthusiasm in talking about films seems as great as when he makes one.

JAMES SILKE: *I've seen all the old films now and want to discuss them. But I want to know a little more about your early career.*
GEORGE STEVENS: That was an awful thing to do to you, all the hours of looking at old film. I couldn't do it to myself, not even out of curiosity. I would like to see some of the older films perhaps, the two-reelers and some of the Wheeler and Woolsey films.

JS: *You became a cameraman in 1922. Do those dates fit the calendar?*
GS: Yes, I think so. I think I did my first work as a cameraman in 1923. 1922 or 1923.

JS: *I saw some early stills of you shooting a Western. It looked almost as rough to make as it was for real cowboys to punch cattle.*
GS: That was part of the fun of the situation. When I was a kid-cameraman, the director of a Western was usually a western guy who could ride and do all those things. I remember the Eyemo camera we used. A hand camera. I remember standing in the back of a buckboard shooting over

From *Cinema*, December–January 1964–65. Reprinted by permission of James Silke.

the horses. We were always doing stunts like that. It was part of the spirit of the thing. It was a lot of fun, and the film looked very good.

JS: *Everybody was involved and everybody was having fun?*
GS: Very good work for youngsters, because these old western boys were pretty fine fellows. It wasn't that they didn't kiss the girl and only kissed their horse and didn't smoke: they were good men and the tradition was such that they wanted to be rugged, responsible. They had an integrity, and being a part of the company was like being on a football team.

JS: *What prompted you to go into movies?*
GS: My father was an actor, a producer-actor, and my mother was an actress. So many people that my father knew had gone into films, but it was not considered the thing to do at that time so my father didn't. But people had enormous successes, like Larry Griffith, D. W. Griffith, who had worked with my father. His name was Larry then. A good many of the stars of Hollywood were family names around the house. Bert Lytell, Hobart Bosworth, Alia Nazimova were all very good friends. But my father stayed on with the theatre business until it finally went right out from under him. It was all films right after World War I. A movie palace was built right across the street from the theatre where my father worked. First one was built on this corner, then one was built on that corner, and the people were going to them in great numbers. I remember my father peeking out through the brass ring before the curtain went up on his stage show, and there weren't many people out front. I remember the last season I was with him and the theatre was just terrible. It was real poverty, there just was not enough money coming in.

JS: *Did you ever do anything in the theatre?*
GS: As a kid I helped my father, setting up the entrances and marking the script and holding the lines. Because he was usually acting in the play and because he also was directing, I helped, holding the script. I also did parts. The last season, I remember very well, was a bad year. My brother and I were pretty big teenagers, I guess around fourteen and fifteen. We would sometimes be given adult parts to do, or we might be given kid parts we were too old for, which was just the worst thing in the world. That was a very bad season. Finally my father came to

Hollywood. He surrendered his pride and came down here and looked up some of his old friends, and they gave him good parts. Over a period of four or five years he starred in four or five pictures, but he gradually lessened out until he was doing only an occasional character part. I was interested in films but I didn't know what I was going to do. I was reading and working on books, educating myself as well as I could.

JS: *What about your education?*
GS: I went to school in San Francisco and studied with tutors. I was interested in photography, too, as a hobby. Film was tremendously attractive to me, and I got a job as assistant cameraman. Lucky. I was on the outside and I got a job with a big company that was about to make *Kismet*. It had been a play with Otis Skinner. I knew a little about what to do that I had learned in a couple of days, so I went home and broke the good news to my father. He raised up and said, "No son of mine is going to be a stagehand!" That was the way he put it. And so we had a terrible battle and I lost and didn't take the job. Eventually I went out and got another one. It led to other work as an assistant cameraman at first one studio and then another, and in a little while I had a profession as a cameraman. That was fine; I found it very interesting. But I was always very interested in plays and playwriting, and studied that.

JS: *Then you've been in the theatre all your life.*
GS: Right. As a kid I was always in the theatre, and as a teenager I worked in it. I listened to the plays on the stages, and I knew how they actually sounded when I read them. I was interested in playwriting. I got books from the library and studied it. Then I began to work as a cameraman, and I got into western work. This was fascinating to me, it took me to outdoor places that I had never expected to be. I learned to do really well, things that before I had only been able to do a little, like riding broncs and riding bareback. I worked on a couple of pictures where we went out to Wyoming and Montana, then to Nevada near where Boulder Dam is now. We were there for six months. There were only two actors with us. It was very simple compared with the way we do things now. When we got off the train, we got pack animals, horses, and went back into the mountains and rounded up a herd of wild horses, and then we went to work photographing the picture. That's

one old picture of mine that would interest me to see now, because I know we did things then with photography that had not been done before, really good things.

JS: *Can you remember the name of that?*

GS: Yes, it had to do with a horse called Rex, and *King of the Wild Horses* was the title of the first picture. Fred Jackman was the director. He had been a brilliant cameraman; he had done the trick work for Mack Sennett. I was one of his two cameramen, his brother was the other cameraman. There were many things that hadn't been gone into in photography then, it had been very harsh black and white. Trick work had been explored but there was not much feeling for the pictorial work. I did a second picture with Fred and his brother and we made a lot of photographic innovations. We used to send the film down to the depot, it went into Los Angeles by train. We had a little electric generator that we cranked with a rope to start our projection machine. When the film came back and we ran it, it was different from anything Fred had seen before. I was fooling with filters and the first panchromatic film, turning the sky black for night sequences, instead of just tinting it blue, and using long telephoto lenses to bring the background up, things that a kid would do. Fred was fascinated with this. When I first came out I was just working for a place on the team; four weeks later I belonged. I was many years younger than he was, but we became very great friends. We worked as sort of a team, after that. To me this was great. I stayed with the camera work and that was the way I came to Hal Roach. Jackman had made these pictures in partnership with Roach who usually made comedies. When Jackman finished at Roach, I stayed on there photographing comedies. As a cameraman, I hated it. It was the kind of comedy you see in *The Nitwits*, the comedian falling into stuff and getting up, it just bored me to death. There was nothing for the photographers to do except, if the comedian was slow getting off, then the cameraman could drop off speed and the comedian would get out a little quicker. Then Laurel and Hardy got together at Roach, and that was great. I enjoyed working with them, because they were inventing something, a new kind of comic film. I had a wonderful period with them.

And then Roach wanted me to direct, which, of course, was what I wanted to do. But he wanted me to direct a certain kind of a picture which just bored me, the kind where everybody is funny because they put on mustaches and all that. He was directing a picture and I was photographing it. In the middle of the day he said, "Why don't you direct this picture?" I said, "Not this one, Hal, something else." He said, "Look, I'm not going to come back tomorrow, I've got other things to do, you take it over." I said, "Not this one." When the day was over, I knew he was waiting for me at the front of the studio so I went out the back gate. He put another fellow on the picture, and the next morning when I came in he said, "What do you want to direct?" I said, "I'll get a story together, and use some characters, more or less natural people." He said, "Okay, go ahead." So I made a few pictures for him.

JS: *Were these two-reelers?*

GS: All two-reelers, yes, comedies and situation comedies. He was not particularly pleased because he wanted a certain kind of picture, more of a gag comedy. Although they worked out very well, it became a contest between us whether I'd make pictures his way or my way. He won and I got fired.

JS: *Were they successful from a commercial point of view?*

GS: Very. Except the second picture I made, I was very unhappy with it. It was one of Roach's type of stories and it was designed to be funny. But with me it wasn't funny, it was grotesque. I had to make retakes on it and I was stricken. I couldn't think what to do. The story department helped me out, gave me some pages of comedy to shoot. It was an agonizing chore, but I managed to do the two or three days' work, which was awful. I learned something, though. I learned it is much too unpleasant a personal experience to go about filming anything that you do not respect. I also learned another lesson. I had used actors in the studio, kind of buddies of mine, who had said, "Now that you're directing, you can use me in your next picture." Some of them who were good friends were not so good as actors. That was a real misfortune.

JS: *When you left Roach, what followed then?*

GS: When I left Roach, Warren Doane, who was Roach's general manager, went to Universal to make some comedies, and I went to Universal, too. That was after an interlude when I was out of work. Banks were closing, it was the time of the depression. But I only had two or three bad months before we went to Universal to do these pictures. I made these comedies in my own way. They gave me a chance to write stories and try them out, stories that bridged the gap between the two-reel comedy and the other fare on the screen, films that had a story and a point and yet had a comedy response. These films were noticed by the people who made the feature pictures at the studio. They were making a picture called *All American* which had to do with a football team, and I did part of that film. That was in 1932.

JS: *It must have been a tremendous step between making a two-reel comedy and a feature film, the pacing of time etc., but there are certain things which I think you did pick up. I didn't frankly see much of what I would call George Stevens's style in* Kentucky Kernels, Bachelor Bait, *and* The Nitwits. *Now, in* Laddie, *there is a certain beginning of what I would say is an interest, a certain essential kind of goodness.*

GS: *Laddie* is the first picture I made that was not primarily a comedy. There was a story to be told that had to do with people. *The Nitwits* was for two popular comedians, Wheeler and Woolsey. *The Cohens and Kellys*, with Murray and Sidney, my first feature film for Universal, was a formula of two comedians that went on and on. After Universal closed down, because of the depression, I agreed to do six comedies for RKO if they would give me a feature to do. The feature was *Bachelor Bait. Bachelor Bait* was not my script, but it was a serviceable script. I think I did very little with it. It was finished in nineteen days. They were making a lot of pictures, so I continued there.

JS: *And you continued to make the features?*

GS: I made the two Wheeler and Woolseys, as I recollect now. Then this little story, *Laddie*. It was from a novel by Gene Stratton Porter. I had more to do with the scripting of this, collaborating on it with a very good writer, Dorothy Yost.

JS: *Well, there seems to be a different visual conception in* Laddie *which may hark back to your cameraman days, and also in* Alice Adams *and in certain sections of* Annie Oakley. *I am referring specifically to what you would call frame composition. I'm sure you've been concerned with this ever since you picked up a camera, with the pictorial look of the thing. It seems to first notably appear in* Alice Adams, *a very handsome film. Also in* Alice *there are two things that seem to be coming out. There's a certain sentiment*

when you switch from the comedy, for instance, very radically and obviously, the affection that you have for it as opposed to The Nitwits *comedy-type of thing, and it shows up primarily with the photography. Of course, Miss Hepburn is absolutely marvelous. Are you aware of this kind of thing?*
GS: That was quite different for her. It was far away from the parts she had been doing to be so purposely romantic and rather simple and sentimental. By nature she was adverse to it, but she fell in with it and loved doing it. She liked the girl that she became when she sat in the swing, and we explored the fact that what she was really becoming in the story was what Kate was herself. At that time she particularly liked to appear very sophisticated, yet she had a very generous heart. She found the whole thing fascinating.

JS: *This is the next thing I wanted to bring out. There seems to be one factor that many directors miss today, this essential factor of the performers really giving more of themselves than acting. The charm, I think, in a motion picture performance comes from the essential character of the performer as opposed to whatever illusionary façade they might be able to create, and it's apparent greatly in* Alice Adams. *It's there in* Swing Time *and, of course, whenever you get together with Cary Grant, and you as a director never seem to miss that element. In fact, even as late as* Giant *when Jimmy Dean is on the screen there's not as much cutting, there's more of just letting your camera watch, whereas with Rock Hudson there's more manipulations with your camera definitely in that area. But your awareness of this whole area seems to be apparent for the first time, I would say, in* Alice Adams.
GS: There were some scenes in *Alice Adams* where the camera merely watched. I enjoy very much the situation when, as the director, I might be busily arranging or managing things, and then suddenly something emerges that's the heart of the matter and I can just put the camera on it and say, "No hands," nothing is guiding it, it's happening.

JS: *It's very apparent in* Penny Serenade *when they're changing the baby. That's the longest shot I think I've ever seen.*
GS: Yes, that ran a long time.

JS: *It was amazing. Is this something you consciously did, or does it come from your interest in just telling the story?*

GS: I don't know where it comes from, but I know how to use it from time to time. With me, that's really the aim in making a picture not to manipulate, not for the audience ever to be conscious of manipulation. Occasionally it could be well to alert the audience to some hand at work, but I've always felt that the other way was the better way. There are those who like to see actresses in roles in which they're playing nothing but a woman acting, and who like to see the tour de force of a director. I think in a film if it's right, there can be a development that is very close to what it would be if it were real life. When a scene is like that, if I can invoke it a few times in a film, it's very satisfactory to me. I remember when it first started happening with me in a film, I had a strong feeling about it, I didn't talk about it, and I tried to bring it about again in a picture. In *Alice Adams* we were close to that in a number of scenes.

JS: *I think that's why it plays so well today. It's very sentimental, it's a very simple story, and one that I doubt is very likely to take place today. It has kind of a period setting.*
GS: It is not true today. I know that environment.

JS: *Did you know it personally?*
GS: Yes. It did exist. It was the environment and it is gone. In our democratic society, which side of the tracks people lived on was tremendously important and an individual's economic background made him superior to another individual who lived on the wrong side of the tracks. It was a rare thing for a poor boy to marry a rich girl and kind of spectacular when it happened. The man was apt to be looked on somewhat suspiciously. A poor girl marrying a rich boy was romantically acceptable if she was from the theatre or glamorous, but for a rich man to find his girl on the other side of town just wasn't the order of things. It wasn't expected to happen in real life, and it didn't happen in the cinema easily, it needed some machinery to bring it about. The machinery to bring it about in the "Alice Adams" character was her deception or make-believe. It was very truly America of that period but it wasn't much beyond that time when these situations were altered entirely. I think the Great Depression helped, because some rich people became poor, and then the war did other things to people and situations. I knew very well from this period Dreiser's book, *An American Tragedy*,

which explored this kind of thing. The Dreiser boy experienced a most extraordinary adventure when he was thrown in with a girl who offered the opportunity for him to improve himself in the social scheme. When we did the film years after the book was written, it was another matter. What happened to him was not so extraordinary; it could happen much more readily; it was no longer such a remarkable adventure. So in the film we really explored the story of looking at society's responsibility to itself and its dicta. There is no moral answer that solves the whole problem of those two people. The only answer is that this should not happen, but the question remains what happens if it does?

JS: *While we're on the social theme, there's a love of America evident throughout all your films. Is this a conscious thing on your part?*
GS: Well, I suppose Americans are the people I most readily understand.

JS: *In* Alice Adams *there's a social theme, and in* A Place in the Sun. *In* I Remember Mama, *there's a definite feeling of social status involved, and in the last half of* Giant. *Now while you seem to have a feeling for this American social scene, you never seem to get off the track of the individuals involved. For instance, in* I Remember Mama, *there's a definite social Swedish kind of environment thing there, a certain economic level. They're talking about money during the whole film, but it never gets away from a wonderful feeling. In fact, that's the only film I can't look at critically, because I get too involved in it.*
GS: I have real affection for that film in certain ways, in some of the most simple ways. I think some of the movement of the film, of the people is absolutely beautiful. It enhances the simplest adventure—it makes romantic a father with a twelve-year-old girl who's going off at night to a poor school—and I think the screen was working to make a lyric of that moment. It was a very simple thing, and I know what it meant to the audience. That aspect of the film has had very little attention. But I know that it has always pleased me very much. I had really retired from films four years before *I Remember Mama*. I had lived some years with films and so I retired and went into the army. I went overseas, I had a deal to go right to Africa where the war was. I certainly didn't know whether I was ever going to pick up a life with films again. Everyone said if you go, you'll be out of it for three years or longer, and

who knows, that might be the end for you so far as film-making is concerned, if you're lucky enough not to get hurt. I was young, a good age to retire, so I retired and went off to the war where things were happening, but I came back after three years and I was happy to resume.

JS: *In a sense, did this getting into the army give you a span, a breather, a difference?*
GS: It must have changed my outlook entirely. Films were very much less important to me.

JS: *Well, they're very different from that point of view.*
GS: Very much less important to me, and yet maybe very much more important to me, in fact—the more I think about it. I didn't know quite what I wanted to do when I got out of the army. I tried to do the kind of picture that I'd done before. I didn't want to go to work right away, but then I got together with Frank Capra and William Wyler. Frank had been home and out of the war for a little while. He'd organized a company and wanted Willy and me to come in with him as partners. I wasn't ready, but because it was Frank and Willy, I went into it. And when I did go into it, that meant that I went to the studio. I hadn't been home long enough to go to a studio. I didn't want to see a studio; I wanted to see the town, the beach, the mountains, the old buildings around town, home, you know. And instead I was in a studio. Frank made the first picture, *It's a Wonderful Life*, and it was time for me to go to work on a picture. I went to work on a comedy, a social comedy, which was to star Ingrid Bergman. It wasn't what I felt to do, but I thought that this was the kind of film that I should do. And Ingrid was ready to do a comedy. Joe Fields, who had written plays which became hits during the war, told me the idea for a story and we bought it. I worked on it with Jo Swerling. Ingrid was playing *St. Joan* in New York and was eager to know about the film. I went back to New York on the train and on the way I worked on the story to finish it.

I telephoned Ingrid and arranged to meet her after the theatre to tell her the good things about the story. But in the meantime I had been thinking—and when we met I was still thinking, and I thought that perhaps our story was not good enough for this sincere, fine artist. "Now tell me about the story," she said with enthusiasm. "Ingrid, it isn't going to be good enough for you and we aren't going to it," I said.

She said, "This is terrible. I've been doing serious pictures, I had hoped you would have a nice comedy for me, and now I am so sad." I said, "The truth of it is that the story just hasn't worked out." I didn't quite know what brought this reversal about. I had done my pictures before on the basis that the principal thing needed was just film, the unexposed film, and the rest would follow. That had been the way that I had always felt before about making a picture. I paused for a moment then to reflect upon the value of self-confidence in work such as this. There were many people who had come back from a long period away in the war and couldn't get going again in this work. Had circumstances changed and shut them out, or had they themselves become different? Now here I was with the most delightful and the most successful star of the time ready and I had a story, but I didn't have confidence in it as a film.

Obviously, something had changed. I came home to the studio and told my partners my conclusions. The project didn't feel right, and it wasn't going to be right as a picture, and in doing it I felt I might betray Miss Bergman's confidence in us. Being the men they were, they understood. I decided I must do a picture that I had a real feeling for, that my present state of mind would allow me to believe in. The play *I Remember Mama* was available, and that was what I undertook for a picture. I knew old San Francisco. I had been raised there, I knew what the city looked like, and I knew who these people were. And it was a story of the confirmed period of the past and disassociated from all of the unresolved present. The next was a matter of great interest to me, a film based on Theodore Dreiser's *An American Tragedy*. I wanted very much to make this film and went about its development with much excitement, and all things came together gratifyingly. It became *A Place in the Sun*. We didn't labor on it too hard; we worked some nights putting the script together, shot it reasonably. Cinematically, it was much the best thing I had done.

JS: *This is the point I was going to get to next in our discussion. Certain things began to determine your style in early films. Primarily you made the early ones, I would say, according to the book. Yet two things stand out. You never missed a good performance, if it was there, a movie performance as opposed to a theatrical performance. In* Swing Time, *I doubt if you shot Astaire in close-up, or even three-quarters, much of the time. Primarily you watched him, because he's so marvelous to watch. The dances are not cut up, they're watched. With Miss Hepburn again, or with Rogers and Stewart in*

Vivacious Lady, *with Beulah Bondi and Charles Coburn, you never miss a trick they give you as cinematic performances. Then with* Gunga Din, *I saw, I think it's the first time, what I would call your sense of montage, and you used it in that film primarily for action. There is a great boisterous, kind of for-fun action, collecting together of shots that establish for the first time, I would say, an overall mood to the whole film. It's just fantastic. It's for action. In* Woman of the Year, *the marriage sequence where she goes to see her father, there's a collection of shots in there where for the first time I begin to see what I call the Stevens's montage, used for purely emotional purposes, not for action. We all know what the action is, but you begin to collect images, one after the other, all pertaining to the emotion within Hepburn: her face, back to the couple, a little closer and you see the old couple touch the hands behind, you hear the words and it starts to build until you have your audience completely with you. I don't see that in other films, except maybe* Penny Serenade *when they take the kid back and you don't show anybody a face, but you show a doll, hands, little pieces of the action that built an emotional situation. And what about* A Place in the Sun?

GS: *A Place in the Sun* has a lot of cinematic revelation in it. Perhaps some of it has become familiar in usage now, but it was adventure at the moment. *A Place in the Sun* is not a restless film. Sometimes it has the strength to be absolutely placid when most of its vigor is taking place, and nothing moves on the screen. And other times when it is not very vigorous, things move deeply . . .

JS: *Do you mean a subject movement?*

GS: The subject, the camera, the light of day, nothing moves. This is a very good variation in this business of tempo and movement. It is at its best when it follows rapid movement and close-up investigation, and then, in a flash, a revelation occurs while the camera stands there spellbound, and the audience is confronted with what is there for them to look at. There's a great deal of that at work throughout the film, a careful consideration of where the audience should be and where the audience should not be. This moves the audience into participation. They gain a feeling of where the film is going and how it's to be revealed to them. Then, if it never quite works the way the audience anticipates, I think the film is functioning at its best. An audience must be a responsive thing. It has a creative function. If it functions as the narrator, that's wrong. The real vigor of the motion picture is lost. The screen itself is basically negative, a white sheet with shadows on it. Only the application of the audience's vitality and creative mental energy create a vigor that brings the nothingness of the screen suddenly to life.

JS: *I guess there would be two things at play there. The audience won't respond unless there's a particular man's whole attitude and love and affection and emotion and talent involved in selecting each one of those things they're going to look at. And that is what I feel, after 1943, that everything on that screen has something to do with George Stevens, each single frame has a look that is George Stevens. All of a sudden the total artistic, poetic aspect of your creativity is on the screen and the audience can't help but react. And as you see, you're not telling them. In the opening of* Giant, *you really don't tell them anything with words, but by each frame you select.*

GS: In *Giant* there is the big house, there is the couple. There is an insignificant character in the background very remotely. I talked to the boys who were working on the cutting. "Don't let the film cut you, don't let the film put you to work putting it together, hold it, make it work for you, make it do what you want it to do, otherwise it will cut you." The insignificant character in the background is a star of the film. We want to get him attention, but we want to do it subtly. If one isn't careful, there could be a close-up on this character; it would be clear that he is significant, that he is the star of the picture. But if the scene is done within the limitations of his own environment, which is just fixing an automobile which doesn't have an engine in it, then from a distance, he has to intrude. The director must not help him; the director must not work the film. But just let the figure intrude from that remote position. He's way off, and he becomes significant. The attention he gets by this means characterizes him. The thing that has been said is: here is the most unlikely, here is the least. Instinctively the audience is exploring, and the response is: this figure is so much the least that an eye should be kept on him.

We have gotten him the attention by two devices which don't alert the audience. A close-up does two things. It reveals what's in the actor's eyes and cinematically it says, *this is significant*. But distance can do the same if the significant figure is arranged in the composition so that the other elements are contributing to it; the eyes of the audience go with the vanishing point to that little figure. And then you give them time.

They wait. Whatever he's doing, or just his hat on the car, preoccupies them. He's way in the background. A gopher could take the audience's eye if it now comes out of the ground. The film stays there for the audience to have time to sense importance. Nothing has told them that the insignificant figure is an important man, but they have discovered that this fellow is of interest, and this kind of work doesn't call attention to any mischief going on; it just lets the audience fall into a response. It also makes the film very innocent of any manipulation.

JS: *In a sense, you would be shooting a montage.*
GS: "Montage," that's a good word to explore. It's occurred to me sometimes when I'm working with film and trying to make alphabet soup into a paragraph of words that say something, that the word "montage" is very misleading. It often means using the filmic equivalent of words, phrases, symbols without design, without relationship, without full awareness of how one affects the other. Sometimes I'll be working on a sequence and someone will say "montage," and I will say, "This is a sequence that is going to require some thought and work." A montage of film is generally illiterate. When I do something with short pieces of film, I do it in such a manner that each piece of film is a statement as related to the other pieces of film. Now certainly the opening of *Giant*, on the surface, is a montage, but each piece of film presumes to relate something or proposes a development. Instead of being an exhibition of film, it becomes a cinematic assemblage. To me, as it is usually defined, montage is film strung together. A number of illustrations make a point, but a montage is film without thought.

JS: *Let's get into the burial scene in* Giant. *This I consider what you would call pure celluloid. You used the term once, I believe. It's not really the performance quality, it's not an actor's quality, it's strictly the director's attitude—the framing of the little boy at the burial, the revelation of the casket behind the train, immobile, silhouetted, and the burial group. And then the services begin. It begins to be a concentration upon life, on the one hand with the little boy, and the yawn, back and forth to the death, the flag and the different sequences, and you carry it right into the birth of the two children—do you remember that?*
GS: I do now, yes.

JS: *The shots of the family where they're getting a little older and grayer, and the one child is born, and the next child is born—tremendous emotional involvement in life and death, and the whole thing becomes a magnificent sequence. You do the same thing in* Shane *with the little boys and the horses, the kids, back to the dirt and into the grave, the people, and it begins to collect what I would say is the pure Stevens's method of making a film.*

GS: That burial scene, that particular scene, comes from a deep feeling. To me, there are moments in a film when there is something for the audience that is valid, that is pure experience for whatever that experience is worth. So you put it there for them to look at. Angel Obregon on a baggage cart is a lot of things to me. I had been taken with a story in *Life* magazine about a ship called the *Honda Knot*, back from the Pacific, where I had never been. On the deck of the *Honda Knot*, in coffins, were the bodies of boys killed in the Pacific Islands during the war. In the European area, I'd been around grave details and seen people put away. But with this awful return, or this august return, there was something I thought we should all pause and consider.

Why the ceremony? If it's dust to dust in Europe and dust to dust in the Pacific, why bring back this ceremonial emblem, these remains? Nevertheless, I think it makes one stop and look at war and learn something about it and feel something about the awful destruction, and I think it has to do with bringing war into the front room, returning it to the home and putting it in the front room, or as close to it as the railway station. An explosive is so far from home, but suddenly the *Honda Knot* delivered one, delivered it with the same message that got you involved in the first place—the flag and the symbolism—and here's what lured you away and here's how you return, or your son returns, or your brother returns. It's a necessary sacrifice, but a great sacrifice it is, and the message it tells is true. That film scene also is true. You don't need to see the *Honda Knot*; you don't need to see the battlefield. The film allows itself one moment to really present a truth.

JS: *That's the one shot.*

GS: That boy on that baggage cart, and when the train pulls out, there it is. Even before the audience has the chance to say, "Don't do that to me," the film says, "There it is, take a look at it." They are made to give that one thing more thought, more attention, than they'd have given it in any other way. It's pictorial bravura, seeing nothing but a baggage car going by, pictorial nothing. Suddenly it becomes like an evening in the west by Frederic Remington. There in the afterglow is Obregon on a baggage cart and you've got to bring it to the audience quickly, let them have it before they have a chance to reject it, let it hold, let them look at it. That kind of thing is good, it's truth, it's an opportunity for truth in this world of fiction and inventiveness. You mentioned the funeral in *Shane*. Again, in this was the base of a lot of what the West was about. People went to a place to live and be buried, they went to become a part of the soil. There was the funeral on the hilltop, and there was the distance where cattle grazed, and then there was the town at the crossing, a western town like western towns were. There were the great mountains that rose behind it. This was all arranged in one camera view, one camera view that had to do with a man being put away in his grave with the synthesis of the whole story wrapped around it. That worked its way into the picture from an idea that came to me in Bridgeport, a small town in California.

Bridgeport, on the way to the Sierra Nevadas, is very unlike other California towns. It's a poor little town but it has a remarkable courthouse, a beautiful white building that was built in the 1880s. About three miles away, in the foothills, there is a graveyard, and from there you can look back and see the town. On this side of the town are the cottages of the pioneer people, the people of the 1880s. A man comes in his front door from a funeral and perhaps goes out the back door to bring in the pail of milk before he goes to bed that night. If he has just buried his mother, he can look up to where she is on that hillside. While he was at the cemetery, he could look back to those beautiful mountains. This is what the pioneers came for, this vast country, and a little cemetery with a fence around it. It's there waiting. Mother, all those who have gone before, are there. It will be throughout his time, and the man can look down to the town and see the house where mother came as a bride, and where he was born and where he was raised. There is a convenience in being able to visually associate all of these essential aspects of life in a frontier world; some of it isn't around the corner or on the other side of town, it's all right there and it's all true. I see that, I know what it means.

JS: *Do you seek this most of the time?*

GS: No, but I see it. There's a significance not to be seen. I feel it, and I want to show it. The *Honda Knot*, the graves detail in Normandy, makes me want that audience to see Angel Obregon's farewell. That remarkable courthouse in Bridgeport, it is still painted nicely, white in front. They hold court perhaps two days a week. When I saw it, the doors were open and I looked down the hallway to the far end and saw two doors. I walked inside. There was the judge's bench, the bar of justice. I had entered through two doors and suddenly I was confronted in this old frontier courtroom with society's guillotine that exists to correct, designed to protect our society, even to the point of taking a life. A device for proclaiming death, the hardest of all machines to operate sensibly.

When I did the film, *A Place in the Sun*, I couldn't get this courtroom out of my mind. The story happens in the country, in New York State. The ambitious boy has taken this poor girl, and he's getting into one difficulty after another because he won't come to grips with his responsibility. He was on top of the world with another fulfilling romance, and now this poor girl demands marriage. It's a holiday and they've gone to this little town. The audience doesn't know what he has in his mind, but he takes her through the door into the courthouse. There's no one there. They walk down to the far end of the hall and there is the marriage license office. As she goes to reach for the door, she sees the sign, "Closed, Labor Day." It's September 2nd. She breaks into tears. She won't look at him. She realizes he's put this over on her. She says, "You knew that," and he says, "Honest, I didn't." He says, "I didn't. You gotta believe me. Gee, you just have to believe me." And she kind of loves him, and she says, "Well, you talked so terribly last night." And he says, "Why don't we . . ." and he's walking along the corridor with her, "Why don't we forget all about this today and come back tomorrow." Then he says, "Let's go down to the lake." She looks up at him and he says, "We can have a fine time." But he doesn't sound just right to me, and I—the audience—watch him and when he stops and says, "Let's go down to the lake," I'm looking over his shoulder. Behind him is the bar of justice, the judge's empty chair. And I know enough about him now to know what he's up to, this "let's go down to the lake." When he is making this proposal he is committing himself to his destiny.

The audience sees that he is going to be back in that courtroom someday, but it's very innocent and there's no more attention to it than that. But an audience doesn't look away. The images are moving fast behind the boy and girl, but audiences catch these things.

JS: *The audience does even if they don't think about it.*

GS: Yes, they accept in this way only what they know is true. There's something else about film. I think all people are very curious about experiences, experiences that in this little life span they may not experience for themselves. A film is a remarkable way for people to experience things they would not have the opportunity to experience in any other way. And I think the best in films occurs when they bring the response, "That's it!" A fine documentary is a wonderful thing, but I think a film is also a documentary when from a fiction piece there is created something that is so much of what the happening would really be. There is a time when the camera offers something in evidence at the climax of a lot of other things, a time when the camera leads and the director is hidden. There is never anything said or done to bring the moment off, it just presents itself. I like a motion picture at a moment like that. Others feel differently, I am sure, but to me that's the best use of the motion picture. I believe that the ethics of a film are to create an actuality. When I am telling a story, how far I may miss it is evident. Because no matter how keenly you aim at reality, you're going to miss it sufficiently that it isn't going to be a look at life. Why look at the screen when you can look next door? I think I am *totally* for reality, but I am aware that I adapt this truth to the romance of the way I would like things to be.

As to the film we have just done, *The Greatest Story Ever Told*, when you come to this story, unless you have spent years in study in this area, you are unequipped to know enough, to understand enough, and to know how it relates to all of its audience, or what is in the varied minds of the audience. When the image comes on the screen, what do they think? How does the figure look? Why is the audience moved? Why do some believe and others reject? For each person, as it is for you and for me, the answers are very personal, very individual. There are enormous aspects of responsibility related to telling this story. This is just the most fascinating adventure in film-making that I could possibly contemplate. Absolutely the most fascinating. In the first place, people love to feel they know exactly what is going to happen in a film. With Charlie Chaplin, you felt that you knew what was going to happen. Except that Chaplin always out-guessed you. When he was surely going to punch a man in the nose, the man punched Charlie in the nose. But the audience always is sure it knows what's going to happen. They're in communion with one another. The first one to laugh, the first one to get the joke, scores a point over the others and he is having a good time. When an audience comes together for *The Greatest Story*, they are really sure that they know exactly what is going to happen, and they must quickly discover that this film presents a new experience to them. We've got to get that audience with this film immediately, and we've got to go ahead with our narration rapidly to make our points.

Once the audience is with the film, then things come easier, and before the film is over, we want the audience completely involved in the story. I can see audiences sitting with this film as though it were a new experience. It's tremendously exciting. We worked very hard on this film to make it into what we consider a play. Two-thirds, or perhaps less, through the story, the Passion of Jesus takes on a dramatic form, becomes a play in itself. But before this point, we worked to create a fine play structure that will take the film up to the Passion of Jesus. This means that all of the early dramatization had to be increasingly on a high key and engender greater response from the audience. We did this in the script. The way we wrote this wasn't glib—write it, then correct it, rewrite it, redo, review, tighten, and enhance. And then consider that result inadequate and perfect it. We think we have a perfect script. Then we question. Should this play have something in the action, something in what is seen, a touch of mysticism, an unreality? But first it has to be happening, it has to be real, the characters have to play. Who knows for certain exactly what things looked like in that world. We know how we *think* they looked or a reasonable similarity. But at the moment I see a happening on the screen, I want it to have a touch of mysticism, a touch of unreality. And yet, if anyone sees it as being unreal, it would miss its point, this fine line drawn by the photography and with the behavior of the people.

JS: *Behavior? Do you mean the physical movements of the people?*

GS: Whatever they do—the way they talk, the way they sit, their movements, their attitudes. In physically putting the film together, all of the work was concentrated on creating an actuality. For instance, the costumes. We almost put guards over the people making the costumes to keep them from looking like they were out of a stereotyped Passion Play. Everyone, everywhere we turned, presumed to know more about the film than they should. And we didn't want the kind of robes that have been appearing in all of the other biblical films past. We wanted costumes to look like something that could have been seen outside of Damascus gate in Jerusalem fifty years ago. Then we could be sure that they would be very close to what they were like 2000 years ago. The problem was to get people to stop doing exactly the same thing they had done last week and to do something different. That's where vigorous work comes into it. But in the end, we had achieved the result that a group of people together looked like a group of people just going about their own business and didn't look like actors in costumes.

When I had gotten them this real, the romantic note could be achieved with other elements—with lighting, with behavior and a touch of visual grandeur. We wanted a feeling of certification by staging the scenes as they were at the time that this story took place. It couldn't be done in Jerusalem today anymore than the Father Knickerbocker story could be done today at No. 1 Wall Street, because everything is so changed. But there are other places that look as the real places did in the time of Christ. There are extraordinary things here in the landscapes that put people to wondering and dreaming about things majestic that could put people to writing scrolls and bibles. The story happened across the ocean, but here we could find settings 2000 years old and older where not a rock has been moved. The story could have happened here, and this helps emotionally. The people acting began fitting into the setting, and the matter of behavior then comes naturally. We worked to arouse that latent something in the viewer's mind that will relate him to the spirit of the theme. The only burden that we basically want to put on him is that he will believe that this kind of feeling exists, that he accept that people thought as the people in the film think. A film has to interest audiences everywhere to be a film at its best. It is now the film's function to ask that the viewer accept the belief in its fullest, but if it can show him through imagery the beauty of the idea, and if it has strength and moments which are at the heart of the matter, then we have done our work well.

The Greatest Story in One Man's View

JOANNE STANG/1965

FROM THE CONCEPTION, through over five years of work to the final print of *The Greatest Story Ever Told*, it is one man, George Stevens, who guided the months of research in the Holy Land, collaborated on the script, shepherded hundreds of actors, extras, and technicians through the filming, and spent a year cutting the picture. It is an undertaking which is awesome to contemplate but one senses—on Mr. Stevens's part—an impatience with awe.

"We know the life of Christ is important subject matter and should be approached with reverence," Stevens declares, "but through the years it has been everybody's privilege to express themselves on the subject. Quite honestly, we felt we were as capable of doing this picture as anyone else working in the medium. So we said the work should be done, wished ourselves luck," he smiled, "and got on with it. As for the particular 'challenges' in making the film, it's difficult for me to talk about them because that implies that they have been met. The film belongs to its audience now, and I prefer to let them judge."

Stevens admits he was intensely preoccupied with the avoidance of both clichés and the usual traduction of the theme. "The basic theme of the story is one which, unfortunately has not always been associated with it in the past. It relates to the universality of men and how they must learn to live together. I think it is a theme of great earnestness and utmost simplicity, and I think all the usual trappings connected with biblical productions—things we have seen in passion plays, films, tableaux, and other demonstrations down through the years—are in

From the *New York Times*, 14 February 1965. Reprinted by permission of JoAnne Stang.

alarming disagreement with this simple theme. We tried, without diverging from the traditional, to think the story out anew and present it as living literature rather than something archaic."

The Greatest Story has received relatively little advance publicity. This has been deliberate. That kind of advance ballyhoo Stevens engagingly describes as "bunkum."

"The usual promotion done for films is very unpleasant related to this subject," he declared. "Furthermore, I don't think it means anything—the usual detailing of all the scenes, the extras, the costumes, etcetera. A worthwhile film collects its own audience. If it's interesting, it will be written about; and if it isn't, you'll be told that, too. Of course," he added, "some people in the industry feel this is an affront to their way of life.

"There have even been a few stories in various periodicals which say that I have told Max Von Sydow, who plays Jesus, not to smoke in public." Stevens looked momentarily droll. "Now, if you know Von Sydow, you are aware that nobody had to tell him what to do. He's an extraordinarily fine individual, and he'd be very disturbed if you did that—and he might ask you how you are doing with your cigarettes, too. Anyway, I think the picture should speak for itself, without the indulgent parents standing around inhibiting reasonable acceptance by their eagerness for approval. In practice this philosophy has worked out very well. Things haven't appeared in print which would have made us very uncomfortable, and we haven't worn out our welcome."

It is perhaps ironic that Stevens had chosen to produce a morality play at a time when many American movies seem preoccupied with smut. He mused about that for a moment, then commented: "I think it's very obvious that audiences really hunger for films which illuminate beauty. I have always believed that they attend movies to gain understanding, to fill in the empty places and smooth over what is painful in their own lives. What they seek, sitting in those darkened theaters, is first identity, then a reason to live. I think film has a unique way of expanding not only the comprehension of the viewer, but providing aspiration for a better life, a finer life."

Stevens used locations in the Glen Canyon area of Utah for most of the outdoor filming of the picture, and some scenes were done in Arizona. "The Jordan Valley, and the country we used for the Jordan

Valley here, were absolutely interchangeable. We wanted to grace the picture with visual beauty, not by artifice, but by nature. Unfortunately some of the landscapes around Jerusalem were exciting, but many had been worn down through the years by erosion and man, invaders and wars, to places of less spectacular aspects. But I am grateful for that trip to the Holy Land. It was unbelievably helpful. You can glean many things by reading, but it's important to pick up a handful of the soil."

During that trip in 1960, the Stevens Company kept a scrapbook log of their travels and in the corner of one page of this is a snapshot of Stevens, in a broad-brimmed Western hat, standing in a rowboat in the middle of the Dead Sea. He looks solemn, and insights into the project seem to weigh upon him. A few weeks ago, while still supervising the dubbing of the picture here, he was clearly exhilarated. "Every day has been an adventure," he said. "When the film is put together, I'll have tremendous satisfaction that the job has been done—to its completion—the way I wanted it done, the way we all visualized it. We are presenting the film with complete humility, without pretensions of associating ourselves with the grandeur of the theme, but merely as artisans, as workmen. But there is no doubt that film is a magnificent medium for expressing these ideals.

"Film fascinates me—that white sheet at the far end of the room and the adornment that is possible to be placed upon it. When something is accomplished visually, I'm moved by it. It delights me to see imagery on film which is moving and significant. It pleases me too, because I know I don't respond to it alone, nor is it only the most articulate people who also respond to it. It is the quiet ones, those silent ones who are the most responsive to imagery that is beautiful on the screen."

Getting the Belly Laugh

ROBERT HUGHES/1967

ROBERT HUGHES: *Can we start with your 1933 film* The Cohens and Kellys in Trouble. *Is it a short?*

GEORGE STEVENS: It was the first film I did that was longer than a short. I had spent a couple of years making shorts—some with Laurel and Hardy—and this film was the bridge for me in getting to longer pictures. I wanted to escape from being a second-class citizen to being a first-class citizen, which meant making longer pictures.

RH: *How did you get the assignment?*

GS: I went to Universal Studios to make a series of films after I left the Hal Roach studios. I think I did about ten films at Universal. We had to get an idea for a film, and then we'd write and cast it. I remember that I wasn't using comedians particularly at that time. The films related more to general fare than to pratfall or stylized comedy. I always found the business of making films with comic intent based on gags to be a very perilous business. If your cast is good and the gags are right, then fine. But if any of the stuff that was designed to provoke laughter didn't come off, there was absolutely nothing there for the audience, and it wasn't a pleasant experience, to say the least. With a nice passive sentimental drama you can take it to a theater and look around during the last reel and if there's a sea of white linen—the ladies' handkerchiefs—you know what the audience is thinking. With comedy, if you get the belly laugh, you know immediately they're with you.

Interview conducted in March 1967; transcript from the archives of George Stevens.

There was a pattern we followed, not that we had been advised by anyone. I think it came more from observation than anything else. It occurred to me that if one has a real story to tell, and one engages the audience as soon as possible, and only then one starts bringing in the gags, then it's all much easier on everyone. The audience doesn't have to sit through an awful half-hour where nothing happens. So I decided that the films I made at Universal should have stories. I just knew that if you engaged the audience with a promise that something would develop, you were in business. If not, you had to contrive automatic ridiculousness continually. Comedy, in this sense, is all about preparation. Things have to be arranged and set up—cause and effect—and if the cause is apparent to the audience, they'll stick with it until their sagacity is rewarded. It's their intelligence that foresees things, while the comic character doesn't. It meant the comedies I worked on were more like the other kinds of films that were running in the theaters. We previewed the comedies before the Garbo and Gilbert films, and it was always reassuring to gain the audience's approval even though we weren't really in the same league.

After this, Universal talked to me about moving over and making feature films. I was very interested in doing this, and *The Cohens and Kellys in Trouble* was the first of them. The film starred Charlie Murray, who was a Mack Sennett comedian, and George Sidney, who's been a theater comedian. They were the Abbot and Costello of their time, which meant everyone expected a gag comedy. There was something of a story, and it did reasonably well, so the company wanted me to continue doing that kind of thing. But this was in the early Roosevelt years, when the Depression was sweeping the country, and the studio closed down for a year. Everyone was out of work.

RH: *And this is when you went over to RKO?*

GS: Yes. They were also in financial trouble, but they needed short comedies. I didn't particularly want to, but they said I could make a feature if I made six shorts. So that was the arrangement. I made the short, and then a five or maybe a six-reel picture. I found out later that the film was made to use up the commitments of actors whose contracts were about to expire, and the idea was to put as many of them into the picture as possible. The film was called *The Great American Herald*, but it was finally released under the title *Bachelor Bait*, for what reason I don't know.

I should say that these first experiences in film excited me greatly. I decided that this was a world I wanted to be a part of. Working with scripts and cameras—it gives me such a pleasurable opportunity to explore and to write and read about things. Every film that I've had anything to do with was a learning experience.

RH: *To go back a little, you started as an assistant cameraman on Laurel and Hardy pictures?*

GS: My father and mother were an acting team. They were always the leading man and the leading lady, so I grew up in that atmosphere and worked in the theater with them from a very early age when I should have been going to school. I got acting out of my system when I was a boy because I had to play parts that I often didn't want to play. I was fascinated by all of it—the sounds of the theater and the audience, their rapture when a play took over and moved them and held them quietly. To me, the sound of a silent theater is extraordinarily important because then the audience is at work all together; they're thinking about what's happening.

I saw films when I was a kid, and I took great interest in them like so many youngsters do, and I couldn't wait for the time when I could make one myself. I didn't quite understand at the time, but the film business was destroying the theater business. We'd move from one place to another because cinema was coming in and it was difficult to make a living in the theater. So my father, who overlooked every opportunity to work in film—he was a little snide about it, even though he had many friends who worked in the industry, including D. W. Griffith—eventually came to southern California to repair the family fortune. He got some good parts and did rather well, so naturally I wanted to get into the business, too. I tried one thing and another, and finally got a job as an assistant cameraman. I was plenty lucky, and it was all very exciting. So I went home and told my father, and he said, "No goddamn kid of mine is going to be a stage hand!" And he talked me out of it, or ordered me out of it. So I lost the job.

Time passed, and I made up my mind I was going to do this, come hell or high water. I got another job as an assistant cameraman and did a few pictures. At the same time I picked up an education. I did a lot of reading. I was interested in plays and playwriting. I also read books about cameras and photography, about chemicals, that a lot of other cameramen didn't. I met a fellow who was a pictorial photographer who taught me a lot. Anyway, I made a couple of westerns for Fred Jackman, who was a great cameraman at the time, and that's what took me to the Hal Roach studios.

The thing about the time I spent at the Roach studio was that actually I hated comedy. As a youngster I'd had no association with it. My father had played in *A Tale of Two Cities* and *Hamlet*, and my mother was a featured actress, but they weren't good at playing comedy or farce. My father occasionally played something that was comic, and my mother always said, "He's not a good comedian." I suppose when I learned not to hate comedy was when it was shown to me by the artfulness of guys like Laurel and Hardy, men who had an extraordinary sense of it, and also from Chaplin. But doing comedy was a good job, and you had a feeling of belonging to something. And then they put the team of Laurel and Hardy together, and I was their cameraman. I didn't know that comedy could be so graceful and beautiful until I met Laurel and Hardy. I didn't know comedy was humane. And I looked at these two men and I realized that these guys understood human nature. By some artistic instinct they had this wonderful business of being in touch with the human condition.

I had worked with each of them separately. It was a good job for a young fellow, a lot of fun. I truly felt part of something. I was very close with "Babe" Hardy, and Stan had an interest in me. I was younger than the other cameraman he'd had. He liked some things I did and didn't like other things, like the stuff that tended to be a little arty. He wasn't too happy when he'd see that coming, stuff that was ruining his comedy. I had to be pretty careful it didn't happen.

I had a theory when it came to comedies that if you do a gag, and you have just a single comedian, he has to be graceful enough to wander into something else, take a lot of time, while the next things are being prepared by what he's doing. But that only works with a fine artist, a real comedian, or with a very well conceived story. If you want to make it easier, use two people, not necessarily working as a team, but alternating. That really helps. But if you *really* want to make things work, take three individuals and never prepare anything. It's always ready to come off the stove. And that's just what we did with *Gunga Din.*

RH: *And you also worked with Harry Langdon?*

GS: Yes. Laurel and Hardy wouldn't make a picture without me, and I got along really great with Harry, so I had to photograph Laurel and Hardy's pictures in the daytime and Harry's at night. It really gave me a lot of confidence. I thought I really had something to offer once recognized stars like Langdon and Laurel and Hardy liked my work. At the same time I was learning a lot from Fred Jackman. He was working at Warner Bros., and when the Hal Roach studios closed for a brief period, he asked me to come down there with him and work as his right-hand man. I learned how to do all this trick stuff. There wasn't a problem we couldn't solve if we just sat down and did it. But I didn't want to stay there with him. I could see that doing this kind of speciality stuff for twenty years would be isolating.

Then one day I was doing a film with a really hopeless director. We had come to an understanding about how to make it come off, but he just couldn't get it together. He was bored with the picture and told me I should finish it as director. I didn't actually do this because I was hopeless and I didn't know what I could do with it. But from that time on I started directing and making the pictures myself.

RH: *You might not have liked the first comedies you made for Hal Roach, but you certainly developed a real feel for comedy.*

GS: I developed an obsession with it. It came about from being in this community where comedy was king. The most brilliant stuff, as far as the audience was concerned, was coming from the comedians—Chaplin, Harold Lloyd, Keaton. They were the flashing stars on the firmament. There was also a whole currency of dull little comedies being made by guys with big shoes and mustaches. Comedy was a way of life, and it influenced people's behavior tremendously. I remember a whole period in my life where everything was a gag. The people I looked up to, the people I was working with, they were heroes because they spun their necktie at a party, and everyone would respond. So we found ourselves always wanting to play out everything as a joke—a very dangerous thing to do, because we looked at everything frivolously.

RH: *When you became a director, did you test the pictures before releasing them?*

GS: As far back as I can remember, the preview was the practice. We had to do it with the comedies. We would time them to the audience's reaction. They'd laugh, and we'd have to lengthen it a little bit to allow for the laugh. Or they wouldn't laugh, and we'd shorten it and indicate that it wasn't so important they laugh at that moment. So I always previewed my films and adjusted them to how the audience responded. But I was never completely pleased with a film that we got away with at a preview because I had seen too many films that preview audiences and critics responded to but that we looked at a year later and weren't pleased with. If you look at most of the films that were acknowledged by the Academy, the most popular and voguish films, they were nothing, while the lesser films often had significant things about them. I've always been tremendously preoccupied with engaging the audiences of my films. Somewhere along the line I got thinking about film, and the only way a film would ever be valid in my mind was that it could be screened and appreciated twenty years after it was first shown.

RH: *Which was the first film of yours that met with this standard?*

GS: I don't suppose any film really meets the standard, but it was always what I wanted to do and what I tried to do. I do remember being in Belgium in October 1944. We'd been up there with the first infantry division, and we got billeted in this building. I remember waking up in the morning and hearing some kids in the street. Now, *Gunga Din* had to do with this cult of Kali, and I hear these kids humming "Kali, Kali." I think, how the hell did this happen? Later on in the day I came upon a theater in this little town the Germans had just left—they might be back next week—and they were showing *Gunga Din*! The kids were more interested in the film than they were in the Sherman tanks going through the damned town. It had really captured their imagination, and something about that film really seemed to stand up. It was a better film than its contemporaries of that year. Over the years I've seen *Gunga Din* survive and others that were much more highly thought of forgotten.

It's the same with *Alice Adams*. The acting was related to real human behavior and not the histrionics of so many other films of the time.

In that film you have a simple guy and an imaginative girl, from simple circumstances. It had to do with people being intimate and talking very quietly. The sound man thought we were crazy. He said, "This won't go by the supervisor—bring the microphone down to where we can hear it." But when we did this he could hear the camera, so we put on a longer lens and moved the camera back. This is all related to why I didn't like comedy. Comedy to me was an invention, and I wanted to put something on the screen as good as some of the better plays I'd seen my father and mother do. I used to sneak in downstairs in the theater and hear plays for a couple of weeks. You get to know when a play is right; you know when the audience is sitting there and liking it. All of a sudden I hear my mother's voice, and then my father's voice, and it's something like I heard in the apartment when they had a quarrel. It was something very real going on up there, and at times like this the audience were absolutely silent. You could hear the audience being confronted with themselves, not a fabrication, not something contrived for their pleasure, but something in the way of education.

This is what the theater does so well. People gathered in a large group, finding a little something about themselves. When the audience was truly moved, it was absolutely quiet. They were in a communion because they were learning the truth about themselves. They were there for discovery, not entertainment. They say film is a narcotic, an escape. But when film was done right, it asked *real* questions: Who am I? Why am I? Why do I do this? Real theater and film is therapy for the audience.

RH: *What was it like directing Katharine Hepburn in* Alice Adams*?*

GS: Kate was a young but grand lady. For me she represented a certain kind of cinema, the antithesis of the kinds of things I had been spending my time on. Katharine had been a great success being strident and strong on screen, but she had never really been feminine before. She had done a number of pictures that were rather stalwart—and had done them excellently—but it was time for her to do something a little different. She'd never played a simple girl in a picture, so her character in *Alice Adams* was a little strange to her, but she got caught up in the idea and loved playing it. She gave herself completely to it, even though she didn't know how she'd come off to the audience. Katharine didn't know if she could get away with it, but found out she had quite a knack for that kind of thing.

She didn't know these kinds of characters at all. Katharine had lived in a family where there was a great deal of activity. Her father was the head surgeon of a hospital who was active in politics, and her mother was an extraordinary woman—a suffragette. It was a big family, and in some ways reminds me of the Kennedys. Everybody was always up to something, and they were always drawn together. Katharine couldn't understand that a girl would have to withdraw into the corner and hope for acknowledgment. In her experience, these kinds of people just didn't exist. She didn't know about the mother worrying about her children or about the financial problems the family was experiencing. I couldn't have made the film without Kate. She's terrific on ideas. She would never wait around for other people to think of things. Kate was never quite so purposely romantic and simple and sentimental, so *Alice Adams* was something a little different for her. It was a long way from the overly sophisticated roles she had been doing. By nature Kate avoided films like this, but was so charmed by the story that she simply fell in with doing it. She had a very generous heart and found the whole thing captivating.

Kate is the most inspiring person I ever met in my life. The figure she presented on screen was a concept. She developed this grace and beauty and moved in where Garbo tread heavily in the imagination of American audiences. Offering no mystique like Garbo had, but offering intelligence instead. It's a strange thing for an actress to present intelligence and make it work, intelligence that had to do with beauty, grace, and just damned good thinking. She was Jimmy Dean-ing before Jimmy Dean ever thought of it, and she wore slacks, too. How she anticipated this era today I don't know, but she did it wearing blue jeans and a sweater.

RH: *Do you remember specifically how you got her to understand about the milieu of her character?*

GS: When we came to a scene, we'd just talk about it. Take the scene when she arrives at the dance. She looks like she doesn't belong. When the music starts and somebody starts for her but then goes the other way, she's hung-up. Once a scene like that is worked out, we know an awful lot about that girl, and so does Katie.

We did have real disagreements about certain scenes in the film, particularly the tragic moments where she wanted to do something that said to the audience, "I am a fine actress," and I wanted her to walk to the window with her back to me so we don't know if she's crying or not—even though we know she's heartbroken. We were in complete harmony before we got halfway through the picture. Think of the scene when she's upstairs with her father. The poor old man is trying to be so goddam nice to her, and he's so hopeless as far as she's concerned. She's looking at him like a horse that's about to have a bear rug thrown at it, and he says, "That's the nicest young man you ever brought home." And she doesn't take an eye off him, and a tear rolls down her cheek. She really knew what she was doing there. She knew he was going to say that, but she can't say, "Daddy, I lost him." I wanted to do the scene again, and at exactly the same moment, a tear again. Thank God for that.

She's an extraordinarily sensitive woman. She would be behind the set just before a take and would be able to walk on filled with the heart of the matter.

RH: *Did you film in sequence?*

GS: Yes. The original script had been prepared by the studio, though it was full of scenes about other people with the kind of talk I couldn't use, so I worked with a fellow by the name of Mortimer Offner to rewrite it. We took the scenes from Booth Tarkington's book—which had a real quality about it that seemed to set itself apart from other fiction at the time—and cut them down, rearranging the plot line. We didn't have the end of the film when we started shooting. The book ends with her going to a secretarial school and starting over again, and we rearranged it according to what audiences wanted at the time, which was the girl gets the boy.

It was actually a very easy picture to make a script out of. Tarkington captured the sounds of those people; he knew how they talked. He knew that from across the street from those little neighborhood houses during the late hours of the night or the early hours of the morning you can hear voices in anger, just like the scene when the old man is so furious with his son because he's made a mistake that will ruin them all, and he shouts and screams. All I had to do with the novel was not ruin it, dramatize it for the screen, and not let Kate Hepburn get in front of the story.

RH: *It must have been a busy time for you, finishing* Alice Adams *and then starting* Annie Oakley *right away?*

GS: We previewed *Alice Adams* out on Sunset Boulevard; it was an excellent, exciting preview. There was a little gathering afterwards for a couple of drinks, and we sat around and talked and had a good time. And I looked at my watch and said, "Jesus, I've got to go home!" They said, "Why?" "Well, I've got to start *Annie Oakley* 150 miles from here tomorrow morning at 8 o'clock, so I better get on the road."

RH: *Was it at this point when you started to gain more control over your own projects and initiating them yourself?*

GS: That's a precarious thing, initiating projects. With *Alice Adams* I didn't come in from left field and say, "There's a wonderful book that should be filmed" like I did with *An American Tragedy*, because Tarkington's novel had already been filmed. But I was a little more cocky at that point. The next film I made, *Annie Oakley*, had a treatment of about ten or fifteen pages, but there was no screenplay. I got together with Joel Sayre and John Twist, and we started to prepare the script. We hadn't a third of the script prepared when we started the picture. If you look carefully, you can see reflections of lesser things gone by. I was continually developing things that would play with the audience because the story was foretold, the ending really was a foregone conclusion. But it ended up being a first-rate film, and modest on cost.

RH: *Were there any projects around this time that you wanted to do, but never did?*

GS: I was in New York and saw Maxwell Anderson's play *Winterset*. It was for me. It was something I really wanted to do. They wanted me to make James Barrie's *Quality Street* with Hepburn instead, and Alfred Santell ended up making *Winterset* the next year.

The other thing I wanted to make was Humphrey Cobb's novel *Paths of Glory*. I have recollections of the First World War, but Pandro Berman was the chap in charge at the studio, and he said, "We can't make this picture." "Why the hell can't we?" I said. "They don't want to make a picture like that about the war." We got it going again, but then they said, "The real reason is that France won't stand for it." I said, "So don't run it in France." The truth was that France would run no RKO pictures if we made *Paths of Glory*. And another thing that the studio said was, "It's an antiwar picture." "Yes! It's true," I said. "It's an argument against war." And they said, "Well, this is no time to be making an antiwar picture. War is in the offing." I said, "What better time for an anti-war picture." They said, "What about Hitler? If somebody doesn't fight Hitler, what will happen?" So there was this big political thing. I don't disagree with the idea that Hitler should have been stopped. In fact, it was another eight years before I realized we should have fought Hitler three years before we actually did.

RH: *Did you see the Stanley Kubrick version?*
GS: No. Not out of carelessness, but I just didn't want to attend another man's wedding.

RH: *How did* Swingtime *come about?*
GS: I worked with Fred Astaire and Ginger Rogers when they were in great vogue. *Swingtime* was made in 1936, by which time they had made *Top Hat, Roberta, Flying Down to Rio,* and *The Gay Divorcee*. They were important stars, and I was asked to do the film. I enjoyed the experience very much. At the time I felt I could do absolutely any kind of picture—I was exploring.

RH: *Was it your idea to cast Hepburn and Tracy together in* Woman of the Year*?*
GS: No, it was Kate's. They met on that picture. I was at Columbia and had made *Penny Serenade*, and Kate had this script which she gave to me. Now, most of the scripts I read are nothing, but for me this was one of the most complete comedy scripts that I'd ever read. It was the only screenplay I ever read that I wouldn't throw in the trash can. I told Kate I wanted to do it, and she says, "There's a problem. It belongs to Louis B. Mayer." I said, "Well, what did you give it to me for?" She said, "I want you to make it." I said, "But how do I make it for L. B. Mayer when I'm working here at Columbia? I have a contract with these people." "Well," she said, "can't we work something out?" I thought about

this, and Kate said, "I have great loyalty toward Mayer. He made *The Philadelphia Story*. And the truth of it is he's got my leading man, too." I said, "What do you mean, your leading man?" She says, "Can you see anybody playing this part other than Spencer Tracy?" I said, "I don't know. … There ought to be a lot of guys who could play this part other than Spencer Tracy." She said, "Well, he'd be wonderful! Let's see if we can work it out." And so I extracted myself from the Columbia situation and went down there to do this picture, and of course it started a great relationship between these two people.

RH: *In 1941, what kind of a position were you in as a filmmaker? Were you able to come to somebody and say, "I want to do this kind of a film?" Or were you assigned a film? What kind of freedoms did you have?*

GS: I had total freedom. Frank Capra had been making films for Columbia under Harry Cohn, and they needed him very badly. I had been making films at RKO, and Cohn wanted to bring me to Columbia. But his relationship with directors had never been good. Leo McCarey, who made *The Awful Truth* for Cohn, was disappointed with the situation, so I told Cohn I wouldn't be able to work with him at the studio there. He said, "I'll make an arrangement with you. You make a picture here, and I'll never speak to you." And I said, "Well, that doesn't make sense. You're a man of enormous experience, you know, and a reasonable exchange of conversation will be all right." Cohn wanted to make an arrangement for a possible three films, but I told him, "Only one film." So we made one film, and we never spoke to each other.

RH: *I understand your camera crews were present at the opening of the concentration camps. I wonder if you care to speak about that experience.*

GS: After seeing the camps, I was an entirely different person. I know there is brutality in war, and the SS were lousy bastards, but the destruction of people like this was beyond comprehension. This is where I really learned about life.

We arrived at Dachau, and I didn't know how many people there were in this place. Some of them had these gray and blue stripes on, most of them had undershirts or whatever, and tons of bandages. They all had malnutrition and sores. I walked into a field of people and looked at them. Half were dead, half were alive, and the live ones had no vitality. In the first place we had to film it, which we did reluctantly. Strange that when you find things at their worst, the most important things to film, you can't do it the way you should do it. The people had gotten rid of the Germans, now what are these other bastards doing sticking a camera in their face. There were certainly a couple of things I should have filmed that I didn't. We went to the woodpile outside the crematorium, and the woodpile was *people*. I remember there was a whole area for Yugoslavs. The only reason I knew they were Yugoslavs was because they had a tag on their coats or a broad purple crayon mark on their chests. There was a dissecting thing in the crematorium where they cut people apart before they put them in there.

I had about eleven guys with me. I don't know how many people there were in the camp. It wasn't as big as some of the others, but everybody's pleading for water and laying there, three guys in a bunk, dying. So I wonder if we can find the medics. We sent a guy down to find the medics, but they have to go and save American lives. So we're bursting through the barracks and go into a room where there's a card game going on between a German major, a German captain, and two nurses. This is the medical outfit, and they said, "We can't do anything. We have no people. What the hell can we do?" "Well, you got water. Start carrying buckets." So we put them all to work, doing what they could do.

We got into Dachau, and it was a bloody mess. We're in these beat up uniforms, and I would come around a block and there'd be one of these poor devils, stricken, standing there shaking and trembling. I've got the uniform on, and he thinks I'm going to do some kind of outrage on him. We take off our tin hats and try to look as little soldier-like as possible, but they'd just stand to attention and salute. You'd go into a block and move down the aisle and everybody is crawling with lice, and your whole attitude is revulsion. You want to lash out, you want to say, "Halt! Get the hell away." They are begging, "Please, water, cigarette, American boy, give me, give me." And you hate them. You look at these people, and you despise them. It was some kind of primitive thing, this feeling. You want to escape them, push them aside, you don't want to catch their lice. You're disturbed by being of the human race. You call these people, you line them up, and you don't know if they're people with families and backgrounds. They're just wretches.

Almost everybody was in shock. There wasn't anybody there I could actually communicate with.

On the third day an Irishman, a sergeant in one of my units, comes over to me and says, "Colonel, I've found the goddamnest thing. There's a whole block of women over here. They're all standing there and hiding. They're in pretty good shape compared to the rest of the people in the camp. They want to have a religious service. Back at the Corps they have a rabbi. Why don't you let them know down at Corps and maybe the rabbi will come up and have a service for these women." The rabbi agreed to come in the morning at ten o'clock. Later in the afternoon one of my men came over and said that the head of the camp—a guy put in by the former prisoners—wanted to see me. He was an Albanian, a politician and a pretty able guy. He says, "Colonel, what's being planned for tomorrow is impossible. You'll have trouble. The people in the camp will not have it. We've got so many thousand Germans, we've got all these Poles, they're not going to allow it. Who would police it?" The next morning the rabbi arrives, and out come the Jews from the barracks. I guess there was about three thousand people—of those that could make it.

RH: *Why did you choose not to make a film about the war?*

GS: Well, it's a funny thing. I quit the film business to go into the army. I wanted to be in the war—I really didn't want to make films at that time. I had the opportunity to go overseas right away if I went into the army at a certain time, as soon as I'd finished *The More the Merrier.* I previewed that picture two nights in a row, then I left for North Africa and never heard about the picture until I was in England three months later.

My agent Charles Feldman told me, "You go in this war, it'll last seven years, and you're finished as far as films are concerned, if nothing worse happens to you." Well, I went in the latter part of 1942, and I came out in 1946, and there was a big question as to whether I was going to make any more films. At least there was in my mind, though I did want to reestablish myself as a filmmaker. I had come back slaphappy, happy to be home, to take off the uniform and put on civilian clothes, to go into restaurants and see people I know, to play football.

I joined up with Frank Capra in Liberty Films. He made *It's a Wonderful Life,* which cost something like three million dollars. So now I'm up, and I chose to do a comedy. I had met Ingrid Bergman in Berlin at the end of the war. She was a bankable star. We became pretty good friends for the three or four days she was around, and when I was back home, she said, "I'll do a comedy with George Stevens if he wants to do one." She'd seen other films I'd done, and so we went to work on this serious comedy. It was a comedy that had something to it. We were having problems with the script; we couldn't really get it together. So I go out to New York to tell her the story, and I'm sitting in her hotel room, and she says, "Now tell me about my lovely comedy." And I say, "Ingrid, we're not going to do it. It's no good." I didn't actually realize this for sure until about ten minutes before this. So I've got to go back to the boys and explain this, that this money has been wasted. There was this play, *I Remember Mama*, that RKO wanted me to do, and that was a long way from the war, and so I took that.

Perhaps *Vigil in the Night* is about the war. In the film, the great irritation of the war overcomes the lesser irritation of their mundane activities, which was something I was really aiming for. It was a tremendous thing, because they brought the head of the company out from New York to get me to cut the line when Carole Lombard and Brian Aherne hear Chamberlain's voice saying, "I am speaking to you from Number 10 Downing Street," which announces the start of World War Two. They wanted the line cut on the basis that America was not in the war, and people would be so disturbed by the picture they wouldn't go and see it.

RH: *The characters in your films are very heroic. How do you get someone like Alan Ladd, who was just an actor up to that time, to exercise a kind of restraint on himself so that he became a very clear, cold, disciplined character, who stands in our imagination as a mythic character, not just as an actor in a western.*

GS: Alan wasn't an ideal man for the role, and he was quite aware of that, so came into it with a wide open mind. It was a real change for him, and of course the actor is always interested in a change. I am aware of this idea you point out about heroic figures. I have often humbled actors, creating stories that will bring a kind of humility out of them, rather than letting them come forth on the screen in their established aura. *Penny Serenade*, with Cary Grant and Irene Dunne, is a good example.

RH: *How did* A Place in the Sun *come about?*

GS: At the time I could see the kinds of films that the public was responding to, things like *It's a Wonderful Life*. I had read Dreiser's novel as a young man and was quite impressed with the hazards of the protagonist and wanted very much to make a film of it. The social scheme isn't crying out for Marxist-Leninism in 1946 like it might have been crying in 1912, or 1922, but we thought the story was valid and that it could be updated to the present era with some reasonable editing, and relate perfectly to what was going on in 1946. But no one wanted it. Paramount had title to Dreiser's novel, and they didn't want the film. They said they had already made it years before as *An American Tragedy*, and it had been a failure. Barney Balaban, who ran the studio, sent me a letter, nine pages long, telling me about how he polled his whole organization and every man—and he named them—said that if we make *An American Tragedy*, it'll be a bust, and it'll put the management in a bad light. They referred to it as a remake. I said, "We're not talking about a remake. The story hasn't been made yet. The theme hasn't been expressed." It was obvious to me that they hadn't made the first film properly. It had been produced at a time when they weren't prepared to undertake a story of that character and consequence. They had done some cut-out episodes from the story, like you do in a funny paper, with none of the nuances or subtlety of the story.

So I went ahead and made the film with real excitement. The whole production was a first-rate adventure. The doing of the script from the novel was very interesting. It had to encompass not only the elements of the story in its entirety, but it should also have the integration of the themes so that it would hold together with dramatic impact. I brought in Mike Wilson, who had worked with Frank Capra, and Ivan Moffat, a guy who had been in the army with me, and we discussed the screenplay.

RH: *Why did you change the names from Dreiser's book in the film?*

GS: We tried to paraphrase the names. Some of Dreiser's names are extraordinarily good, like Sondra Finchley. Highfaluting names that some twelve-year-old or eighteen-year-old adolescent could think, "That's the dream girl for me." Instead of Sondra Finchley I used the name Angela Vickers, which has a ring to it. And the other girl was called Alice Tripp. We wanted to give her a cumbersome name—you don't dream about going down the altar with Miss Tripp. Alice isn't bad, but Tripp? Forget it.

RH: *In your opinion, and in the way you directed, do you think that the George Eastman character in* A Place in the Sun *meant to kill the pregnant woman or not?*

GS: I always had a strange feeling about that story, about the character of this young chap and the circumstances he became involved in, and that it wasn't so much him on trial, as us—the society. I think that's one of the reasons for audience involvement being very strong in the story. I think that at the time, his intention was not to kill her. He did plan it, he did consider it, he did create the circumstances that brought the accident about, but it is still an accident. And who is really guilty here? It isn't that clear-cut. Who is this guy? He thinks to himself, "For years I've dreamed of not being a bum and a street kid. I'm twenty-one years old, and I want to live with the most beautiful girl in the world. I'm just facing the sun so I can have my place in it." With the murder, where does the thought end and the action begin?

RH: *In the book, the girl who gets drowned is a rather different sort—more attractive. The only thing that is going against her is poverty, and conversely the other girl seems rather colder and much less interesting and attractive than Elizabeth Taylor.*

GS: I think that's partly true. The rich girl, in the reader's mind, is a lesser girl, but in the boy's mind, she isn't. She's a society girl, she's bright, and to the boy she is a picture of all that's attractive. I don't know if the other girl is as attractive as you say she is. There's more to it than her poverty. It doesn't appear to me that she's physically charming, beautiful, graceful, or even acceptable in contrast to the other girl. Now, maybe I loaded the dice that way. Maybe in the Dreiser book she's more acceptable physically. I wanted her to appear to be the kind of girl a man could be all mixed up with in the dark, but come the morning wonder how the hell he got into this. If he was married to her, the sound of her voice would be pleasant, he could be comfortable with her, but because he had other ideas, it's impossible.

RH: *How did you decide on the ending of the film?*

GS: This fellow's life is taken at a very early age—in his mid-twenties perhaps. But I think that a young man who has had all these experiences, this extraordinary misfortune of having a mundane ideal presented to him in the most glamorous form—the girl, the money, the success, everything you've ever hoped to gain—it's all an extraordinary experience. So when he walks down to the extinguishment of his heartbeat in the electric chair, this moment let me understand that his life was somewhat fulfilled.

RH: *Your use of sound in* A Place in the Sun *is tremendously creative.*

GS: We used natural sounds for orchestration in the film, the conventional things of our world. When George is leaving the scene of his great misfortune, we hear a group of sirens in the distance far away. They are moving, and there's a question of whether it is in his mind that he hears these things. Then we see that he hears them with an actuality, the feeling of impending doom that is gathering around him—the sirens and the dogs and the railroad. We're never quite conscious of the commonplace sounds, the nice night and morning sounds. We are conscious of them only when they relate themselves to an incident that is in some way memorable. A night that is memorable, a walk that is memorable, an association. We can then think back to accompanying sounds of reality. This is something that's strongly at work in the film. I also had in mind certain tricks, for example the sound of the motorboat. There is an aura of mischief and violence about it. I took the motorboat engine sound out and put one from a Nazi Spitzinbomber, the ones that used to dive on the people on the road when they were trying to get out of France. So the audience is somewhat misled, because when that motorboat pulls away, they are hearing a vicious sound that they might associate with other things.

An interesting thing about the community of filmmaking: I know that the Academy, which acknowledges films for awards, didn't even enter the film for sound. The soundmen thought it was so bad with all these subtle and quiet sounds—they weren't loud or soft enough to please them—though it took awards for photography.

RH: *And the visual style of the film? It seems to be a tremendous advance in visual style.*

GS: I used the camera to create a mood, not in *chiaroscuro* alone, but in the attitude of the camera. I like to see the camera contribute nothing except as a passive witness. When the big moment comes, let it just go back there and not impose itself upon minute investigation of detail to try and proclaim that it is significant.

RH: *Could you say something about the lawsuit that arose due to a television screening of* A Place in the Sun*?*
GS: I sued NBC and Paramount Pictures when they cut *A Place in the Sun*, tailoring it for television. We had designed the film to last two hours. It was designed very carefully with some skill and luck. In many ways it was designed with a form similar to a symphony, with its moods and interludes, and alternate changes of pace. It had real bravura, with naturalist episodes in between. With all that at work, audiences had a real chance to accept the film's meaning, for its meaning to creep into their hearts. With an interruption at the end of an act—just as plays are designed—the story could survive. But on television there were something like forty-two intrusions on the audience's preoccupation with the film. Whatever our film's purpose, it was so hopelessly disjointed and dismembered that it was of no consequence. So I went to court against these two big companies. I sued them on two counts: one, they can't adjust this film because the film was to be made and exhibited the way I put the frames, or the reels, together. They had taken out eight or nine feet of film to screen it on television, and the judge made them put it back. It became a precedent that still exists today.

RH: *How did you get writer A. B. Guthrie to write the script for* Shane*?*
GS: I was trying to figure out who to get for the job, and I had a paperback of either *The Way West* or *The Big Sky*—I forget which—both by Guthrie. I opened it in the middle and found a scene, a group of mountain men sitting around a campfire in the 1830s, and they're talking like GIs. The conversation was flowing freely, and I just hadn't read that in other books of the Western period. I said, "What's happening here? These people have colloquialisms." Some of the stuff in the book was too good to be true, so I called up Howard Hawks and asked him about Guthrie. I knew Guthrie was back there at the University of Kentucky, teaching English literature or something, so I got on the phone and

spoke to him. I told him about Jack Schaefer's little paperback called *Shane*. He was interested, and I said, "I think in about ten weeks we could get something really good done with this." He called me back and said, "I can come out there for ten weeks." So he came out to Paramount and we talked. I gave him the book and told him about some of the things we had in mind. He said, "I've done all kinds of writing. I've never done a script," and he asks, "Can I have a look at one of those scripts?" He got one, and he was looking at it, and he said, "What about this: fade in, fade out." I said, "Well, if you like them, fine, but it's just as well if you leave them out." He said, "Can I take this home to my hotel with me?" I said, "Sure." This was Friday, or Saturday, and on Monday morning he called me and he had fifteen or twenty pages of screenplay for *Shane*. I said, "Jesus, Bud, don't let the writers hear about this. You'll get picketed! You're supposed to talk about this for a couple of weeks and get acclimatized." So we prepared a story outline, and in about four weeks he had the whole damn screenplay, very largely as it was done. Some continuity changes, and editing some scenes out, but the character that came through in his writing was what you see on screen.

RH: *You never made another western after* Shane, *perhaps because the film is the best western ever made. Was it that you never found another story, or did you just want to move on and try something new?*

GS: It's a strange thing, because nothing is more pleasant for me than to be on location in the country that I love, in any of our western landscapes, being out there with a camp outfit and a film company. I had done some work when I was starting in with photography on westerns, and photographing them was the greatest pleasure I had. If I was ever qualified for anything, it would have had to do with making westerns. But as I started working on pictures with people like Katharine Hepburn, I got further away from the thing I really liked to do. You know, the one thing I wanted to do with *Shane* was to show if you point a .45 at a man and pull the trigger, you destroy an upright figure. The first time we hear a gun shot in the film is when Shane shoots at a rock and moves it about two feet. The effect on the audience was much greater than normal because we took the pistol sound out and put in the sound of an eight-inch howitzer canon, alongside a rifle shot. So it had the highs of the rifle shot and the expanding boom of the howizter.

That was the one point I wanted to make. At the time we made this picture there was a great vogue of kids with cowboy hats and cap pistols going bang, bang, bang. I even ran into it in Germany. All the little boys were shooting one another with American cap pistols. At the time, the representation characters in novels, movies, and paintings about the West had injured my sensibilities. In the popular movies we saw western guys with guitars, not six-shooters. In many films the apparatus of the cowboy was very simple. His duds and boots were simple. A leather vest and a hat was the only symbolic adornment that most of those fellows ever had. What I wanted this film to do was catch something of how people looked and lived, their home ways, their manners and ways of doing things, and most importantly the violent character of the six-shooter.

RH: *I wonder if you could talk, generally and specifically, about the pleasures of directing, the enjoyment you get from your work.*

GS: I've always been very fortunate along these lines. I always made pictures for my pleasure, and I don't really have any recollection of getting into anything that wasn't fun. It's so difficult to think of an activity that would give anyone more variety of fulfilling experiences. I think it has to do with one's nature. I have a curious nature, and I'm extremely conscious that more and more audiences reward those films they feel are knowledgeable. My job gives me the opportunity—without being a bum and without people saying, "Why don't you get on with something?"—to sit around the house and read books.

George Stevens

LEONARD MALTIN / 1970

LEONARD MALTIN: *How did you come to be a cameraman at the Hal Roach studio?*

GEORGE STEVENS: I was really a kid at the time, and I had been interested in photography as a kid, as a hobby. I was in the theater world, but looking for a job in the film business. There were no unions, so it was possible to become an assistant cameraman, if you happened to find just when they were starting a picture. There was no organization; if a cameraman didn't have an assistant, he didn't know where to find one. And I learned a little bit about it; I was on a picture for four or five days, had an opportunity to be on a set, and the assistant cameraman kept showing me things. One day I climbed the fence, knowing they needed an assistant cameraman. A couple of days later I was one. The first day or two it was pretty disastrous, but I knew something about photography, and I caught on quick.

When I stayed on with Roach, I started doing some things that they weren't doing because they were very old-fashioned about the photography in their comedies. I worked first with Fred Jackman, who was making pictures with Rex, the King of the Wild Horses. I was cameraman on that, and he was director; his brother was cameraman. I knew about panchromatic film, and they didn't. I had bought the plates from England, a photo store there; we got some extraordinarily good effects and he liked it. I finished those pictures, and there was nothing left to

---

From *Directors in Action,* edited by Bob Thomas (Bobbs-Merrill, 1973; originally published in *Action,* the official magazine of the Directors Guild of America, 1970.)

do but photograph comedies if I wanted to stay with Hal Roach. I hated two-reel comedies, but I got on the Laurel and Hardy pictures and that was great. Roach used to direct a picture every now and then, and he was directing one [not a Laurel and Hardy picture]. About noon he said, "You direct it." He would make one picture a year, and he would always pick the wrong story and get in trouble with it. So I said, "Not for me." I thought what he was doing was silly enough without my trying it. He insisted, and I said, "No, I can't do it, Hal." So he said, "Well, what do you want to do?" I said, "If you want me to direct a picture, let me get my own story, so I'll know what I'm doing." So I did, and it was "The Boy Friends" series.

LM: *So you were writing as well as directing?*

GS: Well, the first thing we did was with a chap named Warren Burke, a bright young fellow who had had a good part or two as a youngster and then there was no more acting for him. He came with me, and we put our first script together. We didn't know too much about it. I photographed it, and it was all right. The next one was terrible. We tried the wrong kind of story, one in which these people were supposed to be comedians rather than people. It was really bad. I had to make retakes on it, and they were the most painful things I ever did in my life. I knew the first thing we did was bad; the retakes were just as bad. I was so agonized, I don't think I ever made another retake on a picture. If there was something I was suspicious of, I'd fix it then. I didn't want the agony of having done something wrong in the first place, and bringing some poor people back with the confidence that you're going to do it better. If they don't rebel and say, "This is idiotic," then you know they're misplacing their trust. The whole thing is appalling.

LM: *"The Boy Friends" comedies seem to have been designed more as silent comedies than talkies; they have great visual ideas, but little dialogue of note. Did you think of them in that way?*

GS: Yes. The only pictures we were making at Hal Roach were silent comedies that spoke; it was just after the transition to sound. The first Laurel and Hardy pictures were really silent comedies. The script was written without any regard for dialogue. The situations were described, with maybe an occasional line. In the silent pictures they'd do the picture and then the titles would be written. Hiram Walker was the title man; he was very funny. So when the dialogue pictures started, the script was written, then it went to Walker, and he'd do the dialogue. So the three or four pages of script were here, and eight or ten pages of dialogue were here; it was sort of non sequitur. The dialogue was usually very awkward in the Hal Roach pictures, including the Laurel and Hardys. In "The Boy Friends" pictures all of a sudden somebody would stop and say something. We depended on situations and sight gags; we were inept with dialogue. The next thing I did was to think of the words as much as the visual aspect. Have you seen any of these "Boy Friends" comedies?

LM: *Yes, I love them.*
GS: Did you see the one with the glider?

LM: *Many times.*
GS: I haven't seen them since I made them. I was telling Hal [Roach] about this the other day. You know, we had no process shots, so how do you pretend this glider is up in the air? How do you get it up there in the first place? There was a cliff, where the top of Marina Del Rey is now, that had an edge where we could move along. We got two big sticks which they use to hoist girders. I hooked the glider on a hundred-foot one, and the camera on an eighty-foot one. We ran it along the edge of the cliff! It was absolutely terrifying, because when it would start to roll, you had the camera boom over you. At least the actor [Grady Sutton] had a glider!

LM: *Your "Boy Friends" films were full of unusual shots. In a football scene you looked at a huddle up from the ground. That was something you just didn't see in other Hal Roach comedies.*
GS: They were so simple. They shot here, and they'd move the camera there. I guess those shots (like the huddle) would look elementary now, because we've all seen that, but they hadn't then.

LM: *Was there improvisation on those films?*
GS: Almost totally. You'd have a scheme of what you wanted to do, that was all. Say Laurel and Hardy were getting out of a car and they go

and ring a doorbell of this house. One of them would go to ring it, and he'd push the other fellow's hand away and say, "*I'll* ring it." He would ring it, but it would be the wrong door, and an old lady would slam the door in his nose. By the time you'd get to the doorway, you'd have fun with the scene.

LM: *How did you come to leave Roach?*

GS: I got fired from Roach, because my films had been turning out better than they had expected. Roach wanted to do a certain kind of picture, like the kind he had started that didn't work. I did gag pictures, because with gags you could get laughs with people who weren't so expert as comedians. I did the football picture and the glider picture, and then one day somebody said that Hal wanted to see me. He told me a story he wanted me to do. I couldn't see it at all, and I'd just started on something else. So I thought it over, and I said, "Hal, I can't do it. I don't understand it." He told it to me again. I said, "Look, I'm working on something else." In fact, I'd previewed this football picture the Friday night before, and it got laughs like you'd get with Laurel and Hardy. He hadn't seen it, and this was kind of an obstinate thing on his part. He was going to do something a certain way. He said, "Now, this is what I'd like to see in this picture." I said, "Hal, I can't do it." A half-hour later the studio manager called and said, "George, I'm terribly sorry. I've got very bad news." I said, "What is it?" He said, "Hal wants to cancel your contract." It was a little shocking to me, but I said, "If that's the way it is, then okay."

That finished me with the Hal Roach studio. It was during the Depression, and things were very bad. Everybody was on half-salary, and the other half went into the studio fund. But if you should leave, you'd get your back half-salary. They gave me a party because I was getting my back half-salary and nobody else was! It delighted Laurel and Hardy, and Charley Chase and the others. "Oh, you lucky so-and-so," they said. Nobody could get a job at that time, but they sent me out delighted, with my back half-salary. I put it in the bank in Culver City, and the building is still closed. Then Warren Doane, who had been manager for the Hal Roach studios, promoted Universal on the idea of making two-reel comedies. Jim Horne, who'd made a lot of pretty good comedies, had left Roach, too. Warren got Jim Horne and me to make comedies alternately. We didn't have much money; there was a small fee for the writer, a little better one for the director. So on Jim's pictures I was the writer, and I'd pick up that fee, and on my picture he was the writer, and he picked up the fee.

LM: *What kind of shorts were you doing?*

GS: We made story shorts. I started making shorts where I would write a story and use more realistic people. I made a picture with Raymond Hatton and Jimmy Gleason, a cowboy story with a baby. Then I did a picture with Frankie Albertson and June Clyde. They'd run for the regular time of shorts, and they were good. After a number of those, Universal wanted me to do a feature picture, to find out what would happen. George Sidney and Charlie Murray were at the end of the line [with their *Cohens and Kellys* series]; they had one picture left to do, and I did it with them. I had no contract with Universal, and they were talking to me about a feature contract. Then they closed the studio. That was the real depression.

But at RKO they had some comedies to make, so I made a deal to do six shorts. I didn't want to make them, but if I did, I could make a feature. Before I finished the six shorts, they had a feature picture they needed somebody to make; I made it, and then I didn't do any more shorts. There's a funny thing about the feature. It was a nice little story, and the writer of the script was pretty good; it wasn't my problem, as most of the others became. But the cast was filled with semi-stars, passé stars, not-quite people, and I said, "Why don't you let me fill in with some other actors under contract?" They said no, I had to use these people, and that was that. So I made the picture, and it wasn't bad. It wasn't until years later that I found out what had happened: RKO had contracts with six actors, each with one picture to go. So Louis Brock, the producer, said, "I'll make a picture and use up all the contracts for you at one time." And that's exactly what happened.

LM: *While you were at RKO you did some shorts with Edgar Kennedy.*

GS: I don't remember how many I did with Ed, but I remember one where he shot a hole in the roof of a train, and it started to snow. We called that the Happy Valley Express.

LM: *I wanted also to ask you about your Wheeler and Woolsey comedies. The end of* Nitwits *is a gag sequence borrowed from one of "The Boy Friends" comedies.*

GS: I remember we did a gag with Wheeler and Woolsey where a kid tried to put together an ersatz machine gun, and we used berries instead of bullets.

LM: *Did you find it a difficult transition from short comedies to feature films?*

GS: It was the easiest thing in the world, because short comedies had to be laughed at. You'd go to the theater and if they didn't laugh, it was deadly. And I had had experience with shorts doing a story. Whenever I got a story into a short—if the story was light and convincing—the audience would stay right with you. You didn't have that awful void if they weren't laughing. So to go over into a feature story was very simple for me, very easy, because the story would work. The problem for me was not to seize a gag opportunity and thus deface the story by putting in some gag business. It was very easy for me to do that; I went for a gag many times when I shouldn't have.

LM: *How did you get the opportunity to move up to such an important picture as* Alice Adams*?*

GS: I did another little picture before that from Gene Stratton Porter's story *Laddie*. It was a pretty good little "straight" picture. Katharine Hepburn was a big star at RKO then, and the studio had this story *Alice Adams*. They were considering two directors, neither one of whom they knew much about. One was William Wyler, and the other was me. For some reason they talked to me about it, and I was very interested. They said, "Would you have a visit with Katharine Hepburn?" I said, "Well, I've got this comedy, and I've got to fix up these gags." I wanted time to read the book. I said, "Could we wait?" and they said, "No, because we have to make this decision between you and the other young director." So they said, "Let's make it this evening," and I said, "Okay, let's make it at her house, after I finish shooting." She was a young but grand lady in the studio, and I was shooting this stuff with guys falling into mortar. I thought, "If Katharine Hepburn sees this, she'll want to air the house out, knowing there's this kind of association." So I talked with

Kate and I hadn't read *Alice Adams*, which was kind of ridiculous. But I wanted to make it and I knew enough about Tarkington to get by. She told Pandro Berman, the producer, "I don't know about that guy. He won't talk about the story." Berman said, "Well, he's a strange fellow; but if he wants to make this picture, he ought to make the picture, even if he has very little to say about the story." They agreed that I would make the picture, and we got along just fabulously. They had a very bad script, terrible script; it was long and didn't seem like the Booth Tarkington I'd read. So I started to read the book, and it was fascinating. We started the picture, and we shot it from the book. I worked with Morty Offner, who hadn't been on the original script. We'd dictate dialogue from the book for three or four pages and do that scene. We finally got a few days ahead. We were often changing it as we went along, until we got to the finish, and we did something a little different there.

As far as making a picture was concerned, I was on very solid ground with a book like that, with excellent actors. Grady Sutton even came into it. We had one casting difference. I wanted to use Frankie Albertson for her brother, and she despised the idea of his being her brother; she wanted a more classical New York actor. But that wasn't the family she was in; this was an American guy who didn't speak too well and got his hair cut in the wrong barbershop. So Frankie did it and did it very well, and she was rather happy with that. Film was never a problem to me as long as you had a story; if you didn't have a story, you were on some tenuous line in keeping an audience with you on the basis of what might happen next—that's always difficult.

Interview with George Stevens

BRUCE PETRI/1973

BP: *What do you make of the concept of time in film?*

GS: When you present a question like that it's certainly something that I never developed my consciousness to, to think of the concept of time in films, because that would have to do with a sort of exploration of films related one to another. As a film viewer or one interested in the film, I'm interested in the film per se, you know? Are you interested in a long book with large paragraphs, or a short book with short sentences, or a long book with short terse sentences? It's something one really doesn't think about. Perhaps in the area we're talking about, it should be related to the usage of the word "tempo."

BP: *I think that's better, because I'm not talking necessarily about one film compared to another, although that's one way that it might be broken down for schematic purposes, but what to do within one film.*

GS: Well, if you broke it down for schematic purposes, you really wouldn't have a response from me on it because I wouldn't want to compare the concept of time in a film that spanned years with the concept of time in a film that took place in an hour, presumably. Because one would be slow-paced and deliberate, and the one that had all the years to span, would have sort of an exhilarated tempo throughout. Hopefully. If it was a pleasant film, it would not have exhilarated tempo throughout but a change of pace—the alternative of a sequence that presents one approach to an event, and then the benefit of the audience's escape from monotony and being put upon by repetitive usage of any kind.

From Bruce Petri, *A Theory of American Film: The Films and Techniques of George Stevens* (Garland Publishing, 1987).

I think the composition of film is very similar to the composition of music; of the variety of music: a symphony, in which the essence of a symphony has to do with its variance—the alternations of time, rhythms, melodic lines, long melodic lines, short melodic lines, escape from melody, and all of those things. A symphony—correct me if I'm wrong—lives by its variation. It lives in its orchestration and choice of instruments. The tempo from one part to another changes by the usage, for example, of woodwind versus xylophone. One would lend itself to exhilarated orchestration, the other lends itself to time. It seems to me in films that the audience, the viewer, not necessarily conscious of it, is terribly aware of the question that you bring up: What is your concept of time?

If the filmmaker's concept of time is in great disagreement with the auditor, the filmmaker's film is in trouble, especially if it's lethargic and maintains that tempo, without the alternation of the dark and the bright. Even though the bright might be for a shorter moment, it lets the body move, and it lets the senses adjust themselves, and it creates what really is the approach to the auditor's sensibility.

BP: *Do you see a change that has occurred with the audience? I mentioned the other day the way I had happened to be with an audience that laughed at Garbo's death scene in* Camille, *and how furious I was at that audience. That's another filmmaker's work, but it's an example of something that time can do if something doesn't come to—*

GS: Now let me put our conversation straight: The film that we're talking about has an audience that's in agreement with it. We're talking about an audience in some sort of a harmonious relationship with the film, or else we're talking about a total waste of time. Of course, a film that agrees with one audience might not necessarily be the mood or the pleasure or the communication that works with another audience. But somehow, films and audiences find one another. I think that's terribly important. Because if we're talking about anything that offers any validity, we're talking about films and audiences that have or do find one another. Now certainly we can't escape the other films, films and audiences that don't agree, and it's a good part of any examination of films. Hopefully we've examined those in private and when we're lending ourself to some sort of examination of the film and its audience, it has to do with a kind of harmony. Not necessarily throughout. But if it's a true, harmonious relationship, it is throughout, because a film is constructed to have the orchestral sense to agree with its audience. That's its basic presumption. And if it doesn't agree with its audience, it's lost. Because there's no changing the audience. Perhaps such a film can find the exceptional auditor that will go along with it, but I'd say he or she is a freak, the film is not made for solitude. A film is made for group assembly, and the assemblage is a part of the communication. Unquestionably, a person sitting with a film alone, one that moves him or—there's an expression I hear eighty-seven times a day—"turns him on," is happier if he's turned on and notices he's in the company of other receptive instruments that are turned on with him. I think that's the audience's virtue. It's one thing to be turned on in your solitude, or turned on in the company of one that you're very sensitive to, or associated aesthetically with, which is a pleasure, but when you get "turned on" together, and that's the last time I use that term, then you have excitement, and it always has been a great part of the theater. Assemblage. This fact that it's fun to be with a lot of people that certify the others' points of view. And I think it has to do with a whole doubt, a whole sense of doubt that exists in the author's mind of a film, not necessarily a book, but of a film. He knows the film is going to be for an assembled group, that the assembled group brings the film to life. A film without the assembled group requires a very extraordinary receptivity in the unit of one, who singularly fills in for the others around him by means of his own assurance—that what he sees is valid; that what he sees is acceptable to him, in his concept; that what appeals to him is good; and that he's not a singular unit. In this receptive sense, that he's human.

BP: *That's interesting in relation to the way I was talking about responding to films by putting other people in the screening room with me when I was watching. I couldn't watch the film alone. That's the same idea I think, that I have to create other individuals, those parts of the audience that agree with me and don't agree with me, and yet somehow we all come together in the film experience.*

GS: I think that's very valid. You know that in a way it's the jury form. A verdict of one, and you're thrown out of court. Seven to five in some juries is an acquittal or conviction. But I think that a film has selected its jury. It's one side of the court, one side of the case, selecting its own jury—and he wants a vote of twelve. If he has one hanging on, one that's not with him, one or two that's derisive, it's a misfortune for the case he's proposed. He either has done the wrong thing, or he has the wrong audience. And it's not much fun for anybody.

This business you're talking about—of a film that's made for one generation, that gets laughed at by another generation—I suppose there's no better effort made for the film medium, to keep it worthwhile, than to have the audience deride that which is inconsequential, or offensive. But I don't think it's valid on the basis of taking a film that's designed for one audience, and presenting it to an audience today, that wants its hamburger and french fries when the film was designed for a filet mignon and brussel sprouts age.

BP: *One other thing it says, too, is that the film is still so immediate that an audience doesn't think of a historical frame of reference for a film.*

GS: Do you mean "historical" in the sense of there's a story behind it?

BP: *"Historical" in the sense of a romantic thirties movie like* Camille, *when the audience had different popular and film conventions than the audience has today.*

GS: I think it's unfair to ask an audience to be aware of the conventions of the film, at its time. I think that an audience looks at the film as a curiosity. And should. Because the audience has a very important adjustment to make. It's a story from another time. And the manners are of another period. The audience has to accept that. The responsibility of the film is to make that valid in another age, which is the time for the film.

To bring the equation to another audience which also is aware that the film technique is a freakish fashion is like a lady coming down the street in 1973, wearing a bonnet, her hands in a muff, wearing high button shoes of the 1912s, and offering those as the fashion of today. Until it becomes totally accepted by a lot of women, it's going to be laughable, and as ridiculous as it is. When a number of them wear them, it's acceptable. So, I think you're asking an audience to be a film auditor: to examine an old film and be aware of the time that it was made and that it was made for the audience of that particular time, when at that particular time its business was conveying a period in France in another milieu many years before. What's really at work here that is false is, Why have anyone look at this old film as anything except as a curiosity? You find the ones that laugh are not looking at an old film as a curiosity, and it can be pedantic to do that and not very pleasant, unless you have a curiosity. So, if there's anyone in the audience that thinks the film should give them some substance, something that's valid and worthwhile, you're giving them a situation that only can cause grave doubts. Something's wrong. Either the fashions of the film of the time are not right to present the fashions of another period earlier than that, which was valid—. You're creating a bridge that's anchored only to one side of the river. The other is without connection with your basic audience, which would be spanned hazardously by any contemporary film that goes back in time. When you go back in time, as you watch this film, you find many, many intrusions of totally contemporary manners, not necessarily clothes, props or so forth, but contemporary manners and definitely contemporary speech, which can be accepted as being reasonable in its earlier context as the translation of a French play into a play presented by English-speaking actors, but the other process is strictly gymnastic. It doesn't belong in any real examination of the purpose of a film, or the purpose of the film audience or the need of the film audience, and the responsibility of the film to relate to its audience.

BP: *One of the things that I noticed that you had done in earlier films that I think has enabled them to live today, more than films that were made at the same time, is that you gave a great deal of attention and care to a specific episode in the film. Especially with climaxes, even if they're comic—like the kitchen scene in* Woman of the Year. *Those are the times when you let the audience respond and react, and the audience is sure of where it is as the scene progresses. I was wondering whether or not that was just a feeling you had, instinctively, as you were orchestrating the film, to use your term, or whether you had any sort of theory about the audience or about putting the film together.*

GS: Very definitely. And it's interesting that you have taken that specific film and that you examine it in this context. Before we go into the business of looking at a film, for instance, this film *Woman of the Year,* which I think was made in . . .

BP: *Forty-one.*

GS: In nineteen forty-one, it's really before we were involved in the great upheaval of World War II, the American side, and all the changes that went with that. So, if we're going to look at a film that reflects contemporary manners, contemporary behavior, and also presumes some sophistication about people with ideas and people without ideas, or with their own simple ideas, as the man had in the play, if we're to make all those presumptions with an awareness of what our audience knows in nineteen forty-one, or what, generally they know, what you're pointing out to me, is absolutely necessary because of the weakness that is inherent in any examination of people's manners at that specific time and of their behavior. We'll have brought it into a point of focus that is a demonstration of manners. It's very precarious as far as the audience is concerned. And I think there's a time, continually a time in the protracted association of that audience with that film, two hours or whatever it is in which there must be a release from their accepting what in many ways could be questionable—this author: probably bright, hopefully brightly; hopefully boldly; hopefully lightly, for their amusement; and hopefully seriously. There's a time when the span of belief will be stretched too far with this pseudo-seriousness, this semi-natural behaviorism, into some sort of a breaking of their attention. And so, what we're doing when we use that comic break, or the light break, that will probably provoke laughter—which it definitely would, because the film would be run with audiences and we'd hear them—and when we break it with laughter, they've made a confirmation of their acceptance.

They have made a commitment in agreement with the film that's extraordinarily true. When they laugh with pleasure at a film that's not a target for laughs, they've made a commitment to the film and you have a little more latitude when you go into the next sequence. As long as they're aware. If they get caught napping, you have them laughing at themselves. It creates relief of the span, hopefully, of belief, of acceptance—making the film into something that gets a very definite verification by the community laughter of the audience. If you had minor doubts or if you were in agreement yet examining yourself—are you the only one having pleasure here with this film?—all of a sudden there's aye, aye, aye throughout the audience on the basis of the unanimity of their laughter. There are two things in the theater you can do that with: a spontaneous round of applause that exists in the dramatic form, from time to time, in the theater, rarely in a film, but it has worked and does work occasionally in a film; but with laughter always in a film, and you create the community of acceptance. Now I present that, when you put me to thinking about this, as a valid technique to be discovered, not to be taught. I've always had an instinct of when to change the mood. I learned from audiences like the five thousand in the Music Hall the first time we were running the film with an audience. I have learned when I was right and when I was wrong. And it's a great misfortune to have misjudged that. You better slip the ship back into the dry dock, put it in the lays, and make some changes, because obviously if under that examination the film isn't working, when you can check it, there's apt to be a lot of other things that are going wrong.

BP: *It sounds as if some of the theatrical background you had might have played a part in that kind of feeling for the audience and for the audience's reaction. I'm thinking of the work that you had with your father and that wonderful anecdote you told the other day of sitting backstage and perhaps doing something else, but you could tell whether the play was working by listening to the audience.*

GS: You put me to thinking—

BP: *From the very beginning it must have been—*

GS: —when I was maybe ten years old—

BP: *—frankly realized.*

GS: —or younger, or older, up to twelve years old, and my folks were in the theater, I spent much time in the theater at night and at matinees in the daytime. I knew their rehearsals. I knew how the play worked. I hardly ever walked out through the drapes behind the box and watched what's going on. I knew what the set looked like; I saw them rehearse it in *A Tale of Two Cities*. I had seen them go upstairs with their costumes, and I saw the orchestra leave the screen room and play the overture. When they opened the door I could hear the audience. When they got back in the pit, they shut the door, and the audience was more muted. They came back in, and the play went on.

And it was as immediately apparent, from where I was, as a view would be to a sightless person, how this play was being approved by the audience. Not only by their response, but by their silence. I think the finest thing to hear with a play that's working with an audience is when the auditorium is totally without people, without breath. Under the stage you hear a line, and something else said, and then a poignant pause when nothing is said, no sound from the audience; and the door opens, and it closes, and she's left forever, from the presence of the man. And the silent audience. You hear a little thump as the curtain comes down, then a crack. And that's applause. All the pair of hands hit at the same time, and that's rare. That's when a play really works. Between that on one extreme and the restlessness on the other, when you sense an audience is restless by the sound of them out front—well, I wasn't thinking about committing any of this kind of thing to memory, but I was tremendously aware of it. I was standing up on a wardrobe trunk with a book. It might be *A Tale of Two Cities* or something else from Dickens. A week before, I had heard the guillotine come down, presumably on Charles Darnay's neck when he said, "It's a far, far better rest I go to than I have ever known." And the silence and the thump and the communication between Charles Dickens to a later-day actor to that whole assemblage of people was total. Good acting, magnificent humanity expressed, a total silence, and then a reluctant beginning of applause and a whacking good applause for the lights coming on and curtain calls. I think that's a big help in relating oneself to the much more indefinite business of putting a film together in an empty room that is eventually going to be exposed to an audience in finality, an audience that's much less communicative than the audience in the theater.

BP: *It is allowed to be less communicative, in some ways, because the film—because many directors confront the audience with the film, and the audience is left there wondering exactly whether or not it can accept it. I think that's one of the things I had mentioned previously about your technique of introducing characters through a window or through a doorway, of giving the audience a chance to meet them a little bit, opening the jewel box just a little, and giving them a peek and then going inside later. It's a form of introduction—*

GS: Well, you spoke about that—

BP: *—that makes the audience more relaxed.*

GS: —a while ago, but I don't respond immediately to it because I think there are probably more than one, maybe a number of reasons that bring that about. We were looking at a film yesterday in which that usage was not apparent because the same thing was at work continually, so that when the scene was important, the people were turned the wrong way to the camera, and a lamp was dividing them, taking up an enormously important position, if the scene was a photographic composition. And something of real interest, if we're interested in the play, is taking place. The two people, a man—a father—and a younger man, sort of taking over his daughter dangerously, but with humility on both people's parts and almost no impossibility of agreement. Now, I'm curious about what is happening—with their exploring the danger line in this relationship. So I keep the camera back in a position that is not going to help the audience too much. Because if these people are exhibiting purposefully, for my purpose in the film, what's on their mind, the audience has a reluctance to be too involved. They sense an imposition on their easy acceptability. I think that has to do with looking at things often from a not particularly accessible point of view, to what's going on. We're curious creatures, and we like to discover for ourselves. In the world that we're living in, in the film, the film is exposing life to you for your convenience. It must, to a degree, and it can under many situations without resentment; but I think it's an enormous waste not to give the audience its priority of discovery, as much as you can. If they have to look a little bit around something, or if they're curious and they sense a little more disturbance in the young man's poise as he tries to be composed and valid, than is apparent from their disturbance, they are fulfilling—and this is a point we overlooked—their creative function. I'll just take that a step further, and I'll say *our* creative function. I think all of us that have been exposed to film, from one time or another, are very often, particularly in our younger years, interested in this film only from our own creative point of view. We're creating this. And in a true sense we are. We're creating this fiction by understanding it, accepting it, and giving it validity because it hasn't validity. It hasn't a third dimension. It's excerpted and put together in various spasmodic arrangements of incidents. It never really works—and I'm thinking of the director sitting there—it never really works for anyone but the audience. The audience must give it the validity. Now, we don't intend to go to a theater and impose upon ourselves the business of giving a film validity. With the things that we seek out when we do, and the things that we discover to be worthwhile outside of distraction, we give the film its validity by our awareness of what is true and what is false and what is significant or dramatic. What has pathos and what is fun. We supply all those things in that empty room behind the sign where it says on the marquee, "The Bijou Dream, Walk In."

This is the point of the audience giving it validity: We certainly are aware that there's nothing quite as unresponsive as a white sheet at the far end of an auditorium and an arrangement of chairs so people can look at the white sheet. Looking at a film or having to do with film, I'm enormously aware of the weakness of that white sheet. It's absolutely nothing. The film moving in front of the shutter presents images that have a degree of reality. You can't touch them. No scent comes from them. They don't approach you. They're abstract. Now this is reality, we presume, in an almost total abstraction. A lot of people are inclined to think of film as a medium in which it has dimensions of reality. One dimension of reality it hasn't got is the important one—the third dimension. Nor the proximity of things behind the foreground figure as much as the proximity from the player to his auditor, because in that is the gain: the distance between the player and his auditor, and not the distance between the player and the background, which three-dimensional glasses will show you with great accuracy. It's terribly exciting if he's in the track and a locomotive is coming out of the tunnel in his direction. It gets more interesting because he's unaware of it. And if he's unaware, maybe I, in my sixth row seat, better start thinking subconscious—I'm exploring the reaction—

BP: *I understand.*

GS: —better start thinking when this locomotive is going to pass him and land in my lap. So, talking about the arrangement of things on the screen and how it relates to a composition of pleasantness. Most importantly, it appears to me, the significant things in films have to do with the relationship between how it's arranged on the screen in relationship to its auditor, and I'm saying an auditor of one. The only plurality I will use will be two: a man and a woman holding hands—they become almost one. And that image, in the view of these two people, makes it exist. They give it credence from their knowledge that it's valid or truthful or acceptable, and endlessly they explore the screen to find this moment in which things are true or valid or acceptable. When they hold the hand of one another and they're related to these figures and they can believe it, fine.

Now, some things will keep them from being related, like the two people are. The people on the screen are totally exposed to the viewer, sitting on exhibition. An actress exhibiting her great sorrow into your face, so you can see her tears roll down—you know she's terribly touched—moves an audience not at all. The restraint of the actress is to conceal her tears. The only way they can be exposed to the audience is if there's a viewer in the background so that when she turns from him, the actress is concealing her emotion from someone in the background. It's so natural that she turned and that I'm confronted with it and play my role, as an audience. I see something that's not meant for anyone to see. Now, hopefully, in the arrangement of things, it could be through a window, it could be some other obstruction, so I don't quite get a good look at her, so that I have to look a little bit around things or do something about energizing my interest. Instinctively, without consciousness, I move to see more. Now an audience alongside of me in agreement with the film will subconsciously make me accept my own acceptance of the film. This is a fine and detailed exploration of an aspect of film that seems relatively unimportant—but is enormously important.

Let me go back to the screen. I say that the white sheet is hopeless. Nothing on there. You turn on the projection machine lamp and it's an affront to your sensibilities; it reflects the light back in your face. But put a shadow in front of the screen, just a shadow, and the light is halfway off your screen. Cover more of it, just the projection light is on it, so there's only a little light in the corner, and then the screen has interest because it gives me my privacy to examine it. Now you start projecting your film and things go on the screen, I mean pieces of film, and their relationship to an audience is orthodox in so many films. There they are, and you look at them—but please look at them from a great distance; or please look at them very close, if it's important; or please look at them from an oblique angle. Not confronted like Reverend Fields in vaudeville. They were the forty-five funniest jokes of their time, triggering the audiences into laughs. This business of giving that screen vitality has a lot more to do with this animate actress up there being flesh and blood and alive as we know it. But as long as we have this single dimension in cinema, the one-eyed lamp out there, give it the quality of obscurity for the audience. The obscurity makes the one-eyed lamp valid, because you don't see perspective with one eye. It doesn't exist. You can draw, as all photography does, the essentials of vanishing points and so forth and so on, but to give it validity to deal with the truth, you're dealing with a one-eyed lamp, you're living life with one eye; and one eye is better than none at all. But the presumption is, that when you look at the screen with two eyes, you can get the full, rounded excitement of being confronted by the images you see with two eyes. I go back to the example of the locomotive. If we're looking at a locomotive coming at us, and both of our eyes are open, we're not going to sit in the track and wait for the protagonist to turn around and see the train coming. We're going to get out of there if we have to crowd everybody out of our row and move. But on account of it being a one-eyed thing, you have to create that sense. You have to create, to give it truth, that sense of motion back and forth. You can get motion left and right and right and left and up and down, but the motion back and forth you have to create.

Now you point out to me, and I'm not particularly conscious of it, that you see things in films that I'm doing or have done that have to do with that kind of thinking and about having it reasonably pleasant to look at. You know that I'm not imposing a banquet feast for you to look at from one end of the table to the other and explore its delights because you're going to consume it. I'm exploring a little fragment of activity in someone's life, and I don't explore it like it's the great moment in the play or that we know what we've come to see, and that it's going to be that particularly great moment, for example, in ballet or opera, where the arrangement of things—the sound and activity and dimensions and presence—are all there to bring us into an extraordinarily realistic association of what we're looking at. You made me pause and think about it. And talk about this—I'm not inclined to ever examine things like that. I know I have often thought and even talked about the white sheet. I know its limitations, but it's awfully hard to be totally aware of those limitations at the far end of the room. Only when you have had a projection lamp over your shoulder and put some images on the sheet, as you run through them in the little room, do you find you're adding very little to the blank frame by what you put on—until something is particularly designed to use aspects of that screen to create visual interest. And more than visual interest, because it relates to some activity that we're aware of that these people, or groups of people, are involved in. The play has to be a very strong play to involve its audience with that. We see more and more usage due to convenience of equipment, of the restless camera, and the focal length moving back and forth and in and out. The camera forever on the move, which artfully done as it has been done, way back to F. W. Murnau in Germany when he made *The Last Laugh,* which was ages ago, but he did things that are done today much more wisely than they are done today. Then it was the first time. But now you have this restless camera in which there are technicians trained to keep a variable going all the time out of the focal length, or panning left and right or dollying in and out. This in a way is taking away from the blankness of the screen; and the movement is excellent if you change the film from a static moment to a variable moment. It's fine as a part of the visual orchestration of the film to have this and the other and another thing, but to make the film continually move along like that is pure escape. And it's an escape from the fact that the audience just doesn't want to look at that plain image up there. Not knowing what to do with it, you keep them moving and the camera moving, to no particular effect. I'm taking a mundane usage of that because we see this kind of thing done brilliantly to bring us into new and unfolding interests. Too often it's accepted as a symbol of modernity to find these devices that work with an able assistant cameraman and a well-balanced operator, keeping this all in at one time. These are the hazards that their director often doesn't get to look at until at least a day or two later. By that time he's done two more sequences of the same character. Pointing that out, I point out that I'm examining the theory, and I'm not offering any one of the variables as an acceptable technique, except offering variables. Except when for some strange reason, and often very effective reason, you want ultimate static and emptiness on the screen: then just let everything sit there.

George Stevens

AMERICAN FILM INSTITUTE/1973

AFI: *Can we start talking about* Gunga Din? *Was the film carefully scripted?*

GEORGE STEVENS: I was doing one thing right after another at RKO with no particular time between pictures. The studio had a script but it was all dialogue. They didn't know what to do with it because it was far from any kind of motion picture. I took one look at it and saw there were no outside scenes—the only thing you saw outside was through the windows of the officers' barracks where some people would ride by occasionally. I was afraid it would be very dreary and just wouldn't have worked as written, so I told the studio that I would take it on but would make a location picture out of it.

The authors were Ben Hecht and Charles MacArthur, two very good playwrights who had written one great play, *The Front Page*—the story of two guys in the newspaper world, one of whom wanted to get married, though his fiancée was the *bête noir* to the other man. Somebody had the idea to do *The Front Page* in India with the same kind of a relationship, so the studio had engaged two stars—Victor McLaglen and the other was Cary Grant—they had each been in a picture for this company a year before, and it had done very well. I wanted a third character so there would be three men, the reason being a simple matter of arithmetic. It was a slight story having to do with action, cause, and effect—action, premise, promise, and result. The third character could alternate with the other two who would be playing against each other, which meant I could be developing the story at the same time. We got Douglas Fairbanks Jr. for the other man. It's so interesting to see a film

---

Interview conducted for American Film Institute, 23 May 1973. Used by permission.

like this play itself out. It gives a real sense, for better or for worse, of the adventure of filmmaking—the opportunity of having resources and the disadvantage of having no dramatic concept of a storyline that is going to put it together.

AFI: *What about the locations for the film? Where did you shoot it?*
GS: I picked the shooting location from an airplane over the landscape of the Sierra mountains in California. I wanted three locations: the flatland, the midland in the rocks, and the higher ground. But the logistics and finances demanded that we do it all in one area, so we put everything in one place and all three locations were within a few minutes' ride of one another. Our star was Mount Whitney, the highest mountain in the United States at 14,564 feet. We changed its aspect by the use of one focal length lens or another. We'd set it back for the parade ground down below and bring it up with a longer focal length lens for the higher ground. It's a rather remarkable area because these are the Sierras at their best. There are these Alabama hills—this strange rugged rock formation that related to places like Persia, Afghanistan, and the Khyber Pass in India. They have taken on a very graceful texture because the erosion has been almost like undersea erosion. These Alabama hills are the oldest mountain range in the world. They have a kind of fantasy and character of their own with these nude limbed trees. As far as I was concerned, that country was very much worth looking at and lends itself to the composition of every shot.

AFI: *Did the writers do much historical research for the film?*
GS: On the screen credit you'll find the name of a delightful fellow and a fine writer named Joel Sayre who wrote for the *New Yorker* and other magazines. I had worked with him on a couple of things. The other writer, Fred Guiol, was a comedy director for Hal Roach originally. We had a start date in three weeks time, and got some books and went to Arrowhead Springs. Joel read the books, Freddie and I talked about things. We needed something to glue this whole thing together and Joel came upon it: the cult of Thugee assassins that existed in India. I knew nothing about it and very seldom ran into anyone who did. We worked it into the theme of the story.

AFI: *What was the budget for the film?*

GS: The studio didn't bother me because I was doing them a favor by taking on this thing. They had so much money for the film, but I figured we needed another $400,000 to take it outside, so that was agreed to. We had to get started on the costumes right away because we would be shooting in three weeks and the script wasn't finished. I went to the studio and ordered costumes for five hundred Highlander foot soldiers who had to have kilts. And of course we couldn't do it without five hundred Lancers too. We wanted to do it with three men of equal rank, three N.C.O.s; so we could only use a work battalion in which there wouldn't be an officer in command. We found a British unit called the Queen's Own Sappers and Miners, dug up the details on their uniforms, and got costumes for twenty-eight soldiers, and three for the sergeants.

AFI: *You say the script wasn't finished by the time you started shooting?*

GS: This particular film, for all the physical activity and vigor of the people, didn't have a finished script. The horrible day finally arrived when we got onto the location up at Lone Pine but had nothing on paper, so we started with a big parade-ground drill. You'll notice that scene where the parade ground is covered with soldiers and they're all drilling without horses. We didn't have enough horses, and one of the advisors—a sergeant major—told me they used to drill on foot. Everybody was there, and I knew it would take a good four hours to get this drill organized so I put this first scene together where Cary Grant meets Gunga Din, who wants to be a soldier like the other chaps—it ends up with Cutter shouting "dismissed" and the Colonel is outraged. It gave us time to organize the parade scene and put a little dialogue together. The scene was scribbled out and the script-girl passed out the three necessary copies, one for herself and two for the actors. After lunch the drill was ready. It was like that throughout the picture: writing a day ahead with me organizing the business from a horse using a public address system, moving around from one shot to another. There was always a script as far as the spoken word was concerned, at least before we started to rehearse a scene.

AFI: *What about the fight on the roof?*

GS: Well, it required an awful lot of shooting—lots of set-ups and explosives—and it took me longer to shoot than anybody imagined.

I know that the studio got terribly anxious, but I didn't need to know anything about what happened in the next reel or the next fade-in to shoot that fight. It took me, I suppose, ten days to shoot it, setup after setup, and it gave Joel Sayre and Freddie Guiol and me time to try to figure a third of our way through the story so we could move ahead.

AFI: *Could you tell us about how you decided on particular shots and how many cameras you used?*

GS: I'd like to, but the strange thing about it is that I was so busy figuring out what we were going to do the next day that today's work was improvised. And the easiest thing of all, when you have great locations, is working out which direction you want to see. We laid out all the sets within distance of our camp so shooting it was never a great problem for me. But it was a problem to keep the audience sitting there for two hours and thirty minutes with a tale as fragile as this one. You depend on the energy of the individual scenes.

We tried to give some romance to the country they were moving around in, the village and this force of Thugee religious cultists. One thing that isn't clear is that the Thugees worshiping the goddess Kali were not associated with other tribes and groups in India. They went their own way and were quite belligerent and self-sufficient. We wanted to create an interest in these people who could ride into town in large numbers, occupy a civilized little village, and test the strength of the military platoon system. But the boys in the uniforms are going to be the ones with the superior skills, and given the presumed attitudes of the audiences that are going to gather for this film, they're going to root for the boys from their own culture. The concept of the film was a kind of "Rover Boys in India" adventure. It's an insular film aimed at a narrow stratum of audience. Anglo-Saxon Krauts, I'd say.

AFI: *What about the structure of the film?*

GS: All the natural responses and basic prejudices create excitement—the cops and robbers, the cowboys and Indians, the cavalry and the American Indians, and Hindus with neck scarves versus white Nordic Aryans. I hope the film exceeds the audience's anticipation with its alternate sequences of promise, development, and conclusion, plus a good storyline that keeps the interest going. The film has a kind of ready-made structure as we move from one thing to another. There are occasional changes of tempo where there is a pause and a regrouping before the film takes off on another thing. I suppose this has to do with not giving the audience too much time to think about things.

AFI: *When producer Pandro Berman was here, he said that you were avoiding him on the set of the film. Was he right?*

GS: I would have been there if he was coming up to bring me some help or something like that, but it happened I'd been working for so many nights on the story and days on the shooting that I was looking forward to finishing the day, and then having Sunday off. I needed that Sunday off very badly. I had sent somebody ahead and got a cabin up the road at Big Pine back in the hills about four miles where I could go when I finished work, flee from there, pull myself together a little bit, and come back Monday morning. All of a sudden I see a studio car drive in while I'm making the last shot. I'm coming down to go to my cabin and it's Pandro. I say, "How are you, Pandro?" and get in my car and leave and come back on Monday morning. I thought he'd stay around till Monday if he was interested in talking, but he didn't.

AFI: *Did you shoot the sequences in the town on location, or is it a set?*

GS: It's a set, we built it—actually we designed it before the script was written. The one thing that's continually at work in the film is the landscape, which is fine to look at. It's organized very well for the camera, much better than many films where studio cameramen went out on location with studio lenses. They used a normal lens and wide angle lens, but I was using long focal length lenses to bring Mount Whitney into the background. These visuals go beyond the set itself, and give the audience something rewarding.

There are two night sequences. The one at the very end with the colonel and the night bivouac were shot out in the San Fernando Valley with bonfires burning. The final sequence of the picture was break of day—a cloudy sky with daylight rising above the campfires. So it's all night-for-night. We used a process shot for the shot of the bridge as the soldiers are crossing it and beneath is a deep gorge. We had about twelve feet of set with a bridge that left room underneath for a solid matte line, and we built a miniature of a canyon to take care of the rest of it.

The Thugee temple near the village was our creation, though the cult really existed in areas far from the most populous areas. They isolated themselves and ran their own country their own way. This temple, this kind of a dream, has a gold dome on it which is not too unreasonable—it could have been a jeweled dome in ancient times. For our purposes it was a gold dome that you could see from a greater distance, and its intrinsic value was apparent to Sergeant Cutter and the other boys.

AFI: *There seems to be many doors and windows in that set.*
GS: It was for no reason other than to relate somewhat to architecture of that hill country south of Afghanistan. It related generally to the Khyber Pass.

AFI: *What do you think of the use of under-cranking the camera when you look at the movie today? I noticed it mostly during the fistfights where it seemed a little artificial. It bothered me because I haven't seen that kind of thing in such a long time.*
GS: Well, you wouldn't be the first to be bothered by it. I wasn't even aware of the scenes where we expedited matters with a slower crank, though I am aware of it in newsreels with our armies marching from World War II in which they're all doing the Hitler rag. Of course it's possible to adjust the camera speed so you expedite things without creating this false choreography of movement. It has to do with the choreography of fistfights where everything works and the right people are hit and laid unconscious, and the other people stand upright no matter how hard the blows are. That's part of the pageant of the film.

Gunga Din, with all the hazards that existed there, had a tremendous excitement about it to me. It's the fact that it's cavalry-scale improvisation—not knowing just how you're going to do it the next morning really keeps you alive.

AFI: *You made* Gunga Din *just before the war. Do you think you would have made the film differently today?*
GS: I made the film long ago, and I made it just in time. Another year later and I'd have been too smart to do it, because the film is delightfully evil in the fascist sense. It celebrates the rumble of the drums and the waving of the flags. No one in modern times has done it as well or

as with as much grace as the British with their uniforms and stiff salutes and all of that. I really got that film done just before it would have been too late. It wasn't a film of any great presumptions either. It wasn't after the Adolph Zukor gold bowl or any of those awards, but it did extremely well with the critics.

AFI: *I know that you started out working with Laurel and Hardy. Could you talk about comedy in film?*

GS: With films like Laurel and Hardy, the filmmaker's existence is maintained by the fact that the audience laughs. If they don't laugh, there is a vacuum, a disaster. Laurel and Hardy were marvelous clowns, but also humanists. Although the story was not always immediately present in their films, their humanism gave them validity. You could watch an audience respond to these structured situations and gags that were premised to eventually evoke a laugh. If the scene gives the audience what they expect, they laugh. So the game is to promise them what they expect, and then give them something they wished they had thought of. Then they really laugh. If it's something utterly beyond their imagination they ask, "Why didn't I think of that?" By laying out the mechanics of it as grossly as this, it doesn't take anything away from its artfulness.

AFI: *Why do you think there are so few contemporary comedies?*

GS: Maybe we're not in the mood to laugh with pleasure at our infirmities as much as we were at one time. Maybe we're curious about frailty rather than thinking it's particularly amusing.

AFI: *You've mentioned the length of your films. After* Gone with the Wind, *and until* Giant, *I can't think of any film that was that long and successful.*

GS: I remember thinking about this business of getting into a film of over two hours. When you do this, the essential thing is to make sure you're telling a story. I watched films that went beyond two hours. I remember being preoccupied with Griffith's *Birth of a Nation* and with *Gone with the Wind*, which was an extraordinarily effective film. I was caught up in it and could have watched even more. What interested me was the similarity between these two milestone pictures: they were both stories based on events in American history—the Civil War, and its aftermath. With both films, the second part—the aftermath—would have been far less rich if it had been by itself.

The original script of *Giant* was by Ivan Moffat, myself, and Fred Guiol. It was based on Edna Ferber's novel and was 370 pages. I talked with Edna and she liked the script very much, saying "You know, I wrote this book twice already and want to write it a third time and fill it out. But I think you've done it with the screenplay." This was a surprise assessment from a lady whose novel we were massacring. After finishing the script I made a deal with Warner Brothers to make the film there. Then Freddie and I sat down and worked on cutting the script. We cut it from 300 pages to 250 pages. I think we got it down to 240 pages.

The film runs three hours and nineteen minutes, and was made to be screened with an intermission. We had worked on the cut to move it along as fast as possible, but I didn't see how we could keep an audience sitting there for that amount of time without an intermission. The end of the first act is when Jett Rink's oil well comes in, and he arrives in his old rickety truck and confronts his rich friends on the porch, salutes Bick Benedict's wife and gets punched on the chin for his trouble and then hits Bick. It was a good act ending: strong and with promise because things were difficult. The next act started with the oil wells coming in. When we first screened it, somehow or other the pace of the picture meant we could get away without an intermission, and we knew we had to run the picture that way. I would have predicted disaster for *Giant*, because when you have an intermission, people go out and talk about it—then they're anxious to go back in and see the rest of it, and it's not such a burden on them. But the picture went straight through, and it's always been run that way. The picture did extremely well—it had far more audience than any Warner Bros. picture ever had.

The structural development of the picture, I believe, is what saves it. It has an excellent structure design, which has to do with the audience anticipating and looking some distance ahead all the way to the finish, which is a reversal on how this kind of story would normally end—the hero is heroic. Here the hero is beaten, but his gal likes him. It's the first time she's ever really respected him because he's developed a kind of humility—not instinctive, but beaten into him.

AFI: *You did some explosive cutting in one scene in* Giant, *something I've never seen, cutting from extreme long shot to extreme close-up. Did that idea come up in the cutting room?*

GS: Long beforehand. I wanted to see this dowager woman, Mercedes McCambridge, on a bucking horse from a great distance—beautiful landscape, straight horizon line, blue sky, and distant image of this contest between a woman and a horse—skirts flying and the horse really breaking it in two. I wanted to go from the extreme long shot to the spur going right into the horse's flank, which—if you had sympathy for the woman—gave validity for the horse bucking like that. In two cuts there's a story—how we contribute to our own undoing.

AFI: *In* A Place in the Sun *you play one scene with Elizabeth Taylor and Montgomery Clift almost completely in large close-ups, and you seem to keep jumping over the line—at least two or three times they're facing wrong directions.*

GS: You mean the cuts didn't make orthodox cutting sense? I don't mind doing that if it's not disconcerting. There wasn't much use then of those six-inch lenses I used in the close-ups. I went from one side of the face to the other and created a tempo—as fast as it could be said it was said. Monty had that kind of emotion that he got steamed up in it. And Liz is so dissolving when she is looking at you.

Now I wrote that scene the night before—put it into a dictaphone, gave it to the script girl in the morning. It was typed up and they each got a piece of paper and the little lady says, "Forgive me, 'Tell Mama,' what the hell is this?" I said, "This is what you're going to say." Elizabeth thought it was outrageous that she had to say that. Reasonable too—jumping into a sophistication that is beyond her sophistication at the time. And also non-sequitur talk because it was spasmodic. I explained I'd like them to get it in their heads, rehearse it off-screen, then get them in there and throw them at one another. I tried to create the fact that this was primitive—the excitement of a preordained meeting where they find one another.

AFI: *In* Gunga Din *you use dissolves primarily for transitions, to lead ahead in time. But in* A Place in the Sun *the dissolves seem to have a purpose beyond merely moving the action ahead.*

GS: In *A Place in the Sun* I was interested in the mood and emotional effect of the story. I wanted to relate the audience to a character whose behavior it might not subscribe to. To bring that about, one must let the audience see his desire. They have to know his need for the thing that—even accidentally—traps him. So how do you do those things? Cinema, at its most effective, is one scene effectively superseded by the next. Isn't that it? The hatchet on the rope and the guillotine falls in the next cut. We have our electricity that creates a current that blows through a film.

When I cut the film I became more and more conscious of the value of one scene against another, and how this spelled something out. I wanted to edit the film together in a way that meant more than the addition of one scene to another. I wanted a kind of energy to flow through. What really interested me was the relationship of images, from this one to that. Shelley Winters busting at the seams with sloppy melted ice cream in a brass bed, as against Elizabeth Taylor in a white gown with blue balloons floating from the sky. Automatically that's an imbalance, and by imbalance you create drama. I'm interested in knowing—as visually as it can be stated—what's on this boy's mind.

The film uses overlapping images in a different way from anything else at that time—dissolves of twenty-five feet with another piece coming in the middle and going out. In planning those dissolves, we used to have to draw them with a pencil, foot for foot. If I wanted eighteen feet, I'd have eighteen feet of scene going out, and then six feet down I'd have the other scene come in. All with a pencil and a piece of paper, and then hand it to a guy to take to the laboratory and you'd see your dissolve a few days later. This point of one visual element against another—it's good cinema. When you see both at the same time in a dissolve, there is a multifold effect. It's all about making sure the film bounces off that sheet and comes to life in the mind of the audience. What is a film outside the audience's mind?

A Piece of the Rock: Interview with George Stevens

PATRICK MCGILLIGAN AND JOSEPH MCBRIDE/1974

THE SON OF VAUDEVILLE PARENTS, Stevens had some experience as a child actor before entering films in 1922 as an assistant cameraman. He became a full cameraman for the Hal Roach Studios in 1924, and in the next six years he photographed dozens of two-reel comedies, including such classic Laurel and Hardy shorts as *Putting Pants on Philip, The Battle of the Century, Two Tars*, and *Big Business*. Stevens is one of the few exceptions to the rule that cameramen never make good directors. When we asked veteran director Allan Dwan why he thought Stevens was able to make that jump so well, Dwan replied, "Because he was a lousy cameraman." Nevertheless, the films Stevens later directed showed the imprint of his cameraman's visual sensibility and the slow, improvisatory pacing he learned while working with Laurel and Hardy.

Q: *How do you think your own films were influenced by Laurel and Hardy?*

A: I was very much influenced by Laurel and Hardy. I remember one time, in *Alice Adams*, Katharine Hepburn, who was the great lady at RKO, had to go to the dance. She got her gown and I put her in a little

---

From *Film Crazy: Interviews with Hollywood Legends*, by Patrick McGilligan, New York: St. Martin's, 2000. This interview was conducted at the Brown Derby in September 1974. A shorter version was published in *Bright Lights* 8 (1979). Used by permission of Patrick McGilligan and Joseph McBride.

Ford with her brother driving. I took a shot of them going down the street and the back wheels were wobbling, which caught the audience off-guard, and there was a very good laugh. Something like that was always going on in those pictures.

I was a youngster when I worked with Laurel and Hardy, in my formative years. The *whole thing* was formative—nobody knew that Laurel and Hardy were going to be comedy stars. They were two hacks around the lot; they had to make a picture, so they put the two of them together.

Q: *Was it the slow pace of their films that made them stand out at the time?*
A: I think a little better definition was that in the fast-moving comedies, the only people that thought about what was happening were the audience, but in Laurel and Hardy's comedies, when something happened, the injured one thought about it, and the onlooker looked at him and thought about how horrible it was. They had the presumption to stop the hand-is-quicker-than-the-eye concept of comedy, which was Larry Semon and the Keystone Kops and all that hurried stuff. Before you could examine the situation, another object had crashed through the window, and it was time for the chase.

The beauty of the Laurel and Hardy shorts to me was their absolute deliberation, their great poise, their Alphonse and Gaston relationship with one another. The Laurel and Hardy concept moved over into other films considerably, with Cary Grant, Roz Russell, Irene Dunne doing the late take and even the double take. That had come out of the personalities of Laurel and Hardy, and the people that worked with them.

Q: *There's a little bit of Laurel and Hardy in the ending of Woman of the Year, the long sequence of Katharine Hepburn comically destroying the breakfast she's trying to cook for Spencer Tracy.*
A: It's exactly that. Those were retakes because the finish didn't work out. I had to put something on at the end.

Q: A Damsel in Distress *was an example of the script not being finished when production started, wasn't it?*
A: It was a very fragile little plot. There was a little story written by P. G. Wodehouse called "Lucky." The character's name was Lucky, and he was a gambler. We had a very fine writer on it, Howard Lindsay, the

playwright who wrote *Life with Father*—a dreary guy to talk to but a funny writer. We gave him lots of time to do it, but after we got so far with this, I couldn't get him on the phone. He left a note, "Dear George, I'm on my way to New York, by way of the Canal. I'm sorry, I'm written out." I had to use Ernie Pagano, a gag man around the place, to work on the script, and I don't know who else [S. K. Lauren]. We got it out the best we could as we went along.

We had a sad thing on that picture, too. This is the first picture that Freddie [Astaire] did without Ginger [Rogers], and it was like Laurel without Hardy. Ginger was a great friend of mine. But she went to Big Bear to do her own picture, and Joan Fontaine was the one who was going to be with Fred Astaire. Now, I never thought too much of that, but I had gone ahead and started to work. Joan had been with me for a little bit in *Quality Street*, and she had done it very well. As far as I was concerned she was in the picture, and we were going to do the best we can, and somehow or other it was going to work out. But Freddie's a great worrier, and he starts worrying about Joan Fontaine. After I've been shooting for about four weeks, Freddie and Pandro Berman, the head of the studio, came down on the set and said, "We're very disturbed about Joan Fontaine. It seems to us that we've got to make a change." I said, "If we take this girl out of this picture, she'll kill herself." They said, "Well, now, that's an exaggeration." I said, "It probably is, but I'm not going to say, 'You can do it, but I'll be elsewhere.' I'll just say one thing: I'm going to stay here and you're not going to do it. We've got to put her through this picture." I can understand Freddie, he's great artist, but she was a girl with problems, you know, she cried and all that. So they went back and they thought it over, came back with a plea for Ruby Keeler, somebody that could dance. I said, "I'm not going to take this girl out of the picture." Freddie said, "Go ahead, let's make this goddam picture." They were right, she was the wrong girl in the wrong spot. She never knew that they wanted her out of the picture, or she would have collapsed.

Q: *How did you deal with her limitations?*

A: It wasn't *Top Hat*, but Freddie's got a couple of good numbers in the picture. We did that thing on the creek with the fog and [cameraman] Joe August ["A Foggy Day"], that's one of the popular numbers. She didn't have to dance at all; he did all the dancing. And it was very pictorial. We did what we could to make the picture work.

Q: A Damsel in Distress *was the first film you did with August, who was certainly one of the greatest cameramen in the history of Hollywood. [They also worked together on* Gunga Din.*] How was he to work with?*

A: The interesting thing about Joe August was that he was almost totally inarticulate. He always had to sort of pantomime anything he wanted to tell you, with sound effects. Having done that sort of work myself when I was young, I had developed the same [way of communicating]; I thought it was style. I realized that Joe August was an artist. And he's as mute as Quasimodo. So the fact that he's tied around the larynx gives all the muscularity to the visuals. That's one of the reasons why the John Ford pictures he photographed are so beautiful. Remember *The Informer*? And Joe was no Irishman. But he knew what went on in that Irishman's mind. He had a boldness. He always liked to do something that was dangerous. He liked the chance that he was going to blow it. One time I was with him on the stage, and we needed more set. The production manager and the grips are thinking about how they are going to get a piece of wall in there. He says, "Forget it." And they say, "What did you say, Joe?" He says, "Forget it, I'll take care of that." Then he throws a streak of light along the wall, high, and turns a light on up there and makes it accent the set. He could be so tremendously good.

Q: *You often take a long time cutting a film. What kind of working relationship do you prefer with your editor?*

A: My problem, from the first two-reeler I ever made, was that I had to get up in the cutting room and put the damn thing together so it could be shown. You can't ask another man to unsnaffle all the parts of things that were done, sometimes with hope, other times from necessity, and other things that you've shot and would like to work in, if possible. I really rehearse on film; you know, your film stock is the cheapest thing you have. So I get a rough cut that comes along from an editor when I'm doing a film and I suffer through it and then go to work and apprise him of what those cuts are. To make the film work, to create a kind of poetic feeling, well, there are a thousand ways to cut it.

It's like playing a piano—the right notes to hit, and the emphasis, the *sotto voce* and the *profundo*. We used to get very good directors, great directors, way back in the history of film, like [D. W.] Griffith, who knew how to wake an audience up and make film work as it had never done before and, in some ways, hasn't since.

Q: *It is true that you came onto* Gunga Din *at a late stage?*
A: We were fighting for our lives to make a film of that. [Ben] Hecht and [Charles] MacArthur had written a script, and Howard Hawks was going to do it. But Hawks had gone on, and they asked me if I would make a picture of it, because they had two actors, Cary Grant and Vic McLaglen, who were committed for big salaries. I liked the [Rudyard Kipling] poem—I knew it wasn't related to the picture at all—so I read the script. It was impossible, because it was all inside. "The Rover Boys in India," but inside the barracks, and that was just not going to work for the Occidental audiences. If they are going to be in India at the Khyber Pass, the audience is going to want to see something of it.

I said, "I want half a million dollars to take the story outside. I want to do it on three elevations, the desert, the semi-uplands where there will be rugged rocks, and high ground. And I want a third character so the story will move." This was rather a sleight-of-hand trick, you know. So I said, "Doug Fairbanks, Jr., is free. Doug has his disadvantages. He's rather stiff. But this is going to be a very light role, and to lighten him up will be fine."

Q: *How did you get a final script?*
A: I called Joel Sayre, who is a good short story writer. Joel and Freddie Guiol and I went to Arrowhead Springs and took two stenographers and we walked around there and read books for three or four days. The poem was about a true cult that existed, and the history could give us some authenticity. Then I went back to the studio and got Perry Ferguson, who was my art director, and we got airplanes and took to location. Fred and Joel arrived on the location the day after we started shooting, they stayed at the hotel at Lone Pine, and Joel did some very good writing.

Freddie was going to shoot the second unit for the battle scenes and I would take care of the close-ups. But Vic McLaglen used to get loaded at this saloon, and one day Freddie—he was always a very tough guy—met

Vic in the street, stopped him, and said, "Where the hell do you think you're going?" Vic said, "Anywhere I damn please, laddie." And Freddie says, "To hell with that, McLaglen, you're going to bed. You have to work early in the morning." So Freddie put McLaglen to bed. But Freddie's a terrible bottle man—and he was so exhausted he himself went up to have a drink. And by daylight they're putting *him* to bed, you know? Before we got to the end of the picture, Freddie developed a heart condition and he had to go home.

So I was stuck up in that country with Joe August, one of the best cameramen in the business, but we had no second unit, and it meant doing everything ourselves, you know. The studio was after me to come on in to do the interiors, but I figured I just couldn't get it all in the studio, because on location I had alternatives. Finally we got to the point of, "What do we need to do next in this damn picture?" and so help me, we couldn't think of anything. So I called the studio and told them we were coming in. I guess there were some heads shaking, but our footage was quite good.

Q: *Where did you shoot the ending?*

A: We did that down in L.A. It was my idea to put in the recitation of the poem. We got a beautiful night and a beautiful dawn, out in the Valley somewhere where the real estate is now.

Then we had to cut the picture. I had an awful lot of cutting to do with all this battle stuff, and Jesus, some guy at the studio put it together and it didn't make any sense. So I went over to the comedy department and got an old-timer who used to be my comedy cutter to come over and cut the battle scenes together. "You know," he told me, "You can cut no piece of film shorter than six feet." I guess there's a lot of guys he's told that to who believed him; it was one of the rules handed down from Zion. Eventually we had eighteen-frame cuts all the way through that picture, and I had to lose him; he wouldn't cut a piece of film that short.

Q: *Cary Grant did some of his most offbeat work for you, in* Penny Serenade *and* Talk of the Town*, as well as in* Gunga Din.

A: I didn't want to do gag pictures with Cary Grant; Cary was doing nothing but comedies then, so I wanted to do something slightly different. Cary was always ready for everything. In *Penny Serenade*, we had a scene where he goes in to see the judge about the child. His heart is breaking—and he's got his hands in his pockets. Cary didn't hold up on doing that at all. Not any more than he held up on putting his hat on backwards in *Gunga Din*. He thought that was pretty silly, but I suggested he do it, and he did it. Jesus, we put a bellboy's uniform on him, the dress uniform of that particular group, but I don't remember Cary having a problem with it. That's the way he was. And Cary's perfectly capable of suggesting changes in the script and coming up with ideas.

Q: *Whose idea was it to put Spencer Tracy and Katharine Hepburn together for the first time, in* Woman of the Year?

A: There's a lot of indefiniteness about that, but I'm quite sure it was Kate Hepburn.

Q: *Why do you say that?*

A: Because that's the way Kate gets things done. Kate is terrific on ideas. She doesn't wait around for people to think of things. Kate brought the script to me and asked me to read it. It was forty pages short of conclusion; it was never concluded until we got down there shooting. I said, "This is great, Kate, bring it to Columbia. Let's do it." She said, "You missed the point. I've already promised Louis B. Mayer because he's been very helpful to me." I said, "I can't do that, I'm making pictures with these people down the street." She said, "Oh, those things aren't so difficult to solve," So I went down to Metro to do the picture while Harry Cohn burned. I never went back to Metro after that—too damn many story conferences. Good directors didn't stay long at Metro.

Q: *What about Clarence Brown?*

A: Clarence Brown is a *marvelous* director.

Q: *You directed Jean Arthur in* Talk of the Town, The More the Merrier, *and her last film,* Shane. *How was it working with her?*

A: She was interesting because she seemed to be rising above her personality. Anytime she has a charge to make against someone or a defense of something, it always seemed that she felt herself dangerously exposed, kind of heroic in the most ordinary circumstances—even if she had to put her left hand out in traffic in order to turn. You had to treat her like a child when you directed her—she was terribly anxious about everything.

Q: The More the Merrier *was your last picture before you went into the service. What was the shooting like?*

A: We had fun on that picture; I don't usually have fun on a picture because I've usually got a little too much writing to do. I knew it was my last picture, and I had a limited time to do it, and I wanted to enjoy it. There was no question about how it was going to develop; it was going to develop well. And the circumstances, as we went along, just folded in nicely.

For the first time in years, I took a film out for a preview and didn't take it apart. I'd put in for a commission, I got it, and the war was on in North Africa. It's hard to get a fifty-yard-line seat like that. So I took one more look at it and left it like that; I never saw the film again. I never heard anything more about it except once, in *Yank* magazine, in Algiers, I read where the film was up for the New York Film Critics' award.* That was good news but I knew it was a good film. Anyway, by then I was out of the film world, entirely.

Q: *Could you relate some of your experiences during the war?*

A: One night, we were over in the Persian Gulf, which is the dullest place in the world, and there were a hell of a lot of troops in a sort of amphitheater; there must have been twenty thousand guys there, and they were going to see a movie [*I Wake Up Screaming*]. It was a film you would avoid seeing. I was very fond of Betty Grable, she was a friend of mine [Stevens directed her in *The Nitwits*, 1935], but she was in it, and it just wasn't my cup of tea. But I sat there with twenty thousand other guys and I saw the Passion Play. I had a *tremendous* experience watching this film. There was a good sister and a bad sister, and the foreign chap,

---

**The More the Merrier* was voted Best Film of 1943 by the New York Film Critics' organization.

and what do you think? It's the bad sister who's winning all the way. Betty Grable is the good sister, because she's glossy and cute and the GI's dream. Everybody just sat there and there was a catharsis.

The film was fifty times the weight on each individual it was designed for, at home in their own theater, where this game was happening in their own lives. Here, they're cut off from all of that. Here, like in a cathedral, it brought them face to face with simple experiences that can be the most profound experiences in a person's whole lifetime. I was a little bit more of a person after seeing that. It was more important than B-47s or B-48s or the Afrika Korps and divisions moving and casualties going back, that ridiculous life which was the most exciting life in the world at the time.

I had gone to Africa because the U.S. Army didn't have any war films. The British came out with their *Desert Victory* and we had nothing. I got into a division outside of Algiers and I picked up Bill Mellor, the cameraman who was with me for so many years. Here they had a Hollywood cinematographer and they didn't know whether to send him into the MP or the KP or what. They gave us some tanks, with powder men—that's one thing the army had, great powder men—and we were shooting over the moving tanks with stuff blowing up in front of them. We were down there about two weeks, sending it back to Frank Capra to make the American film on the African war [*Tunisian Victory*].

In Algiers I got in to see Eisenhower. It was two days after Rommel surrendered, and I asked Eisenhower if he had talked to him. I would have liked to hear about it. I never forgot this, especially when he was running for president. He says, "I'm here to kill Germans, not to talk to them." That s.o.b. You've got to be eight years old, you know, to have your masters talk to you like that and not have it have an effect. All the time he was campaigning for president, many a time he was on the television, I would make that remark and lose a couple of votes for him. It wasn't enough.

Q: *Your unit filmed concentration camps at the end of the war in Europe. Can you talk about that?*

A: We cut the barbed wire to go into Dachau, and that's beyond description. The only way you can talk about it is in photographs. I came around the corner of a building, in my uniform, and these people were absolutely in a stupor or a tension of fright. They were wearing these dismal stripes, they know it dehumanizes you. As I came around the corner, this one man went from however he was to the most upright figure. I guess he'd been a soldier. He was terribly thin. And he was so stricken: he saluted me. It oppresses the individual that he's reacting to, terribly. I mean, you must be one of the worst kind of villains of all time. I guess if they didn't salute just right or stand at attention just right, or breathed wrong, they would be on the woodpile. So help me, where they had the furnaces and all of the bodies are stacked up, they had sort of a purple ink on them that said "Pole" or "Czech." Some had tags on their toes. There was an enormous gassing oven; at first we didn't know quite what it was. And there was a tremendous pile of bodies on one side of the building all during the time I was there, although they were burying a lot of them.

Q: *How do you think your war experiences affected your later work?*
A: It causes a most profound adjustment in your thinking. I don't suppose I was ever too hilarious again.

Q: *You did direct a comic segment in* A Miracle Can Happen [*a.k.a.* On Our Merry Way] *for United Artists in 1948, didn't you?*
A: [Producer] Benedict Bogeaus was trying to get a lot of stars in a picture, a *tour de force*, and he offered a fantastic sum if I would do a comedy sequence. It had Jimmy Stewart and [Henry] Fonda—I'm smiling already. And I wasn't worried; these people are going to be funny. We put a Laurel and Hardy thing together. With ordinary actors I've tried this, and it's like playing music without an instrument, but these guys could do anything. We had a hell of a lot of fun and I got my feet wet, you know, making something which was hilariously funny without a note of humor in it. It was all structural. My partners got $50,000 for it and that did my ego some good.

Q: *You mean Frank Capra, William Wyler, and Sam Briskin, your partners in Liberty Films. Why did you become involved with Liberty Films after the war, instead of returning to Columbia?*

A: Harry Cohn and I had met in Paris at the end of the war and he said, "Now are you coming back to Columbia?" What could I say in the Ritz Bar in a worn-out uniform—no, I'm not? I guess I said yes; well, this created undying enmity between Harry Cohn and me, the only guy to ever tell me I broke a contract. And he meant well, he was just being sweet, and I should have come back with Columbia, because I had had wonderful pleasure working there. But Frank Capra had organized this company, and Willy [William] Wyler was there, so I joined them.

For some crazy goddam reason—maybe I wanted to throw a slow, soft pitch or something—I got hold of a comedy story that was very interesting [*One Big Happy Family*] and I went to work on it for Liberty. Ingrid Bergman had agreed to star in it. I worked on it for some time, and I didn't mind that it wasn't maturing well because I've had that happen before. Ingrid went to play Joan of Arc in the theater, but I really wasn't getting anywhere with this comedy. We had taken Sam Briskin as a production man, a partner, and he kept an eye on things. Frank was making a big picture [*It's a Wonderful Life*], and I had to cosign all the checks. I never paid for so much snow in my life. I said, "Jesus Christ, I wish this Capra would stop spending so much money, I've got a sore arm." It got to the point where Sam Briskin said, "Ingrid is *so* interested, I wish you could go back and talk to her."

I said sure, that's just what I need to do. I'll quit fooling around. But by the time I talk to Ingrid, I'll have to tell her something that's pretty good. So I didn't take the airplane, I took the train. I figured that would give me plenty of time. I met Ingrid in the alley after the play. She asked me, "How are we coming with our comedy?" I said, "You know how these things are," and we had a couple of drinks at "21." And she said, "Well, you have to tell it all to me." Ingrid pours a little cognac, she's all smiles, and I said, "Ingrid, we're not going to make a comedy." I felt like a heel. I said, "It just isn't working for me." I just didn't see a goddam funny thing about it at all.

Q: *How did you settle on* I Remember Mama *then?*

A: RKO was going to make it with Irene Dunne, and somebody there suggested that she should talk to me about it. I'd seen the play with Barbara Bel Geddes in New York, coming out of the Army, and it was a nice little play. It was set in San Francisco and I was a kid there during that period. I thought it would be fun to reconstruct the period. It was at the most a play that committed itself only to mom and the family. Nothing contemporary.

As time went on, however, I kept feeling I should do a picture about the war—all the other guys had done or were doing pictures about their war experiences, [John] Ford, [John] Huston, Wyler, and so on. And here I was avoiding the subject. Until I found *Shane*—it was a Western, but it was really my war picture. The cattlemen against the ranchers, the gunfighter, the wide-eyed little boy, it was pretty clear to *me* what it was about.

I did an unusual sound effect in that picture. In most Westerns, you know, people are shooting off guns all the time, until you don't even notice it anymore. I wanted people to be really jolted out of their seats the first time Shane uses his gun. It didn't happen until maybe an hour into the film; I very carefully kept gunshots out of it up until that point, to make the first one more emphatic. So I got a little cannon, put it right off-camera, and when Alan Ladd fires his gun, I had them shoot off the cannon and it made a tremendous roar.

Q: *Why did you choose A. B. Guthrie, Jr., to write the script of* Shane?

A: Bud was a good friend of mine, but he was very reluctant to be down in this area. In fact, they were doing *The Big Sky* [based on a Guthrie novel] across the street at RKO, and they had tried to get Bud to do the screenplay. I had read a couple of Bud's novels; he was the only damn Western writer that could get Westerners to be as voluble as GIs were in bull sessions. He wrote GI dialogue. It wasn't just a parody of other Western writers, who seem to put a limitation on how much a man should say. I'm not sure those Westerners were so much silent as their authors were ungifted.

I called Bud in Montana, told him what we were doing, and he said, "I think I'd like to do that." I said, "C'mon down and see if you can." So he came and I told him what I had in mind; I hadn't lined out the thing completely, but I wanted to get him interested in it. He said, "Well, what do you got for me to read?" I gave him this Jack Schaefer paperback. This was a Friday afternoon. He said, "Do you have any film scripts around?" I said, "Oh, gosh, there are a lot of those around this building." He said—he was teaching school—"I want to see how the form goes." I said, "Let's leave that for later as far as I'm concerned." He said, "Well, I'm curious, so let me have one or two of those, will you, so I can take them to the hotel over the weekend." So he did.

Monday morning, Guthrie walks in the door, and he's got a script of the paperback. He has something like thirty-seven pages, numbered, with the fade-ins, and the fade-outs and the cut-tos. I said, "Christ, don't take this over to the writers' building—people see you walking in with a script on your first day, you'll have a bomb over there in your room. The theory is you stooge around for about ten days before you get started." It was damn good. Bud Guthrie was putting himself into another tale, and it was excellent. But we got about two-thirds of the way through the script and Bud had to go back to Montana. School was starting up again or something. He rushed through some sort of a conclusion, and let it ride. I never really got through a whole script before we started. After we straightened out the chronology, the night before or sometimes during the day, we were still doing some scenes to finish it. But by then I knew the actors, and it's very easy to write to the actuality of a situation.

Q: *Alan Ladd as Shane was such a marvelous piece of casting but unconventional, particularly because he was so short for a Western hero.*
A: It was an interesting thing for the picture because he didn't tower above the others—the mountains did. We kept him as high off the ground as possible so he wouldn't be dwarfed by people.

Q: *One of the greatest and best-remembered shots in* Shane *comes at the beginning, when Ladd is riding toward the homestead in long shot and a grazing elk in the foreground of the frame lifts its head just at the perfect moment to frame the horse between its antlers. How did you do that?*
A: I sent out and got a little elk and a couple of bucks with big spreads. What I did was to have the buck alert us to the rider; the figure on horseback comes straight down—it's not across the screen or interesting, just progression, a kind of monotony. We lined it up and then worked with this buck to have him in the foreground; we had some dry stuff or weed up there that he went after a few times. We rehearsed with Alan Ladd and got Ladd back—he's going to move along at a signal—then we moved the camera over to where the buck was grazing. There's a fella out there, hidden back in Ladd's direction just out of frame, with

a bucket and some rocks in it. During the take the fella shook the rocks; it sounded a little bit like rain. Once we did it and the buck looked toward the rocks. We took it again, the buck stayed right there with his good downtown hay (it's unusual for him), and on cue, a silent cue, we watched this rider come along.

And it was a coincidence, the horn was right in the middle—it was awful good. So I decided to shoot the works, since I was going to get lucky. I kept it quiet, let the animal graze, got Alan all the way back there, silent signal for him to start on, silent signal for the camera, he's coming on and pretty soon we call up the cue for the buck. Not quite. A little more cue. He looks up, and Alan is right between the antlers. Three takes. You're either going to get it or you're not going to get it. There's no use persisting; it just had to work that way.

Q: *Do you think that in period films, such as Westerns, using long takes and a deliberate pace, as you do, helps draw the audience into the period subconsciously?*

A: I suppose that's true, and not only for the Western, but of all films to some degree. Perhaps it's more true of the Western—I never thought of that. I know we are often aware of the *aficionados* of rapid cutting; we're not always aware of people who like to see things build suspense or energy with one particular piece of film. It's related to music or painting, the arrangement of film, and it has an enormous effect on an audience. They never relate to it as being devised, any more than I presume I'm seduced because Renoir devises the composition of what he shows me in a painting. I know he sweated it out, erased it, but he got it. There's no question about it, there's the grand man.

It surprises me how well audiences, also critics, reward a film that has that kind of thing in mind, by design, not because it just happened. Sometimes we find really fine quality in a film by looking at it, looking at it, and then looking *back* at it—why, this darn thing's designed as the *Bolero* is designed! In one of those long takes, the camera gets rooted in one place almost as if it has discovered something of extraordinary importance. It doesn't move in to examine it closely; it draws the audience in to make an effort to see more. The audience must explore it, discover why there is this muted telling of some significant point. They're in a position where they can have a reverential look at something.

Around this point in the interview, Stevens looked at his watch and asked, "Anybody want one for the road?" So we ordered coffees, bringing the interview to a rapid conclusion. That meant we had to rush over most of his other work in the 1950s and 1960s (A Place in the Sun, Giant, The Diary of Anne Frank, The Greatest Story Ever Told) *if we were going to draw Stevens out on his current attitudes toward the film business and on his last film.* The Only Game in Town. *On that film, as on* A Damsel in Distress, *Steven's loyalty to an actress took precedence over more sensible casting.*

Q: *How did* The Only Game in Town *come together? Casting Elizabeth Taylor with Warren Beatty was rather odd.*

A: My wife and I wanted to go to Paris. And Liz Taylor is a buddy of mine. And Warren Beatty is a real buddy. So I read the script [by Frank Gilroy, based on his play]; it's a very nice little script, but it's none of my work. I wasn't going to take that script apart and give it more size and space, but I liked it. And I said I'd do it. Frank Sinatra and Liz Taylor were part of the deal. That script? I don't see how they made the deal. Now with Liz and Frank Sinatra, it's all going to be considerably unreal. But if you can make it pretty real, it's going to be rather interesting. Frank Sinatra fell out of it, and I called up Warren. He said, "Count me in." Now I've got a problem. It won't work. Liz Taylor won't work with Warren. And so we've got to use this other girl, what's-his-name's daughter, the Irish director's daughter—

Q: *Mia Farrow [daughter of the late John Farrow]?*

A: Mia, yeah. She's fragile. She's sensitive. She can stumble around and be a little problem. But with Warren Beatty in this fragile little piece, it could have been real. Warren is very human and bucolic in a young domestic situation. I said, "Okay, we can still do it." Dick Zanuck, who was running Fox, flew over to Paris, and I said, "We can't do it with Liz Taylor, now that we've got Beatty. The frank thing to do is just to tell Liz that it will not be good for her and put Mia Farrow in the picture." Dick is all for it. Well, somebody told Liz. Jesus, 1:55 A.M. and somebody's banging on my door at the Georges V. In comes Liz. She says, "Well, I've had a new experience in my life, thanks to you. I've been fired from a picture." I said, "What do you mean, fired?" "You don't want me in this picture." "Certainly, Liz, I want you in the picture. But the way this is working out, you don't want to be in this picture. It's not right. Taylor and Sinatra fine—Taylor and Beatty no good. Drop Beatty, get someone that goes with Taylor. But the two are not going to make the story believable." Well, anyway, by that time Zanuck has come. And she gives him hell and all of that, and then [Richard] Burton arrives. They all arrive in my room. I said, "What the hell. Let's go ahead and do it. See what happens."

Q: *Do you have any plans for more films?*
A: No, I haven't. I'm avoiding it. Too many other things to do. Too many other things to read. Do you ever read scripts? They're impossible. "Cut to close-up," scenery, meaningless description. Jesus, some of them are written in Arabic. I can't follow a script at all. I got tangled in a couple of projects and I always managed to get out—I was going to do *Butch Cassidy*; I got pretty mixed up in that, then I said no. And then *Funny Girl, Nicholas and Alexandra*—but some how or other I always escaped confinement. I'm escaping it with more adroitness now.

Q: *Don't you have any desire to make a film?*
A: Here's the story. Here's exactly the story. I'd *love* to make another film. But the way I make a film, nobody would make it. You know, it means I've got to take three years, two years anyway; I've got to work on the story. If somebody just gives me a script—I've done this, I've gone nuts—I won't shoot it. It's no picture. And then I've got to go to the bank.

Jesus, one time when I was doing *The Greatest Story Ever Told*, I needed $5 million to continue. I was shooting process, which is the dullest thing in the world, and they told me that the Bank of America people are coming. We had a lovely restaurant at the old Ince studio, but I called the property man over and I said, "I've got to have lunch here on the set. Put a bridge table over there, chairs for the four of them, get ham and cheese sandwiches and coffee." We all sat down for lunch and they knew I needed a lot of money. We started with radishes or some other very unpopular vegetable. One smug little guy, a fat older guy, takes a deep breath and says, "You know, every time I get in this atmosphere of a motion picture studio, I get terribly, terribly uneasy. All the things which happen in this business give us problems." I said,

"Brother, do you remember 1930? Everything I had in the world was in the First National Bank in Culver City. Did you notice when you came by that building it's still empty? I still haven't got my money out of it. I get terribly nervous when I eat with bankers, so we are both going to have a nervous lunch." Exactly as friendly as that. This is the guy who took my $2,100, everything I'd saved from Laurel and Hardy and the other pictures, and blew it. I brought that up a couple of other times. Jesus, bankers! We got our $5 million.

Talking of The Greatest Story Ever Told *put Stevens in mind of Carl Sandburg, who worked with him and James Lee Barrett on the script, receiving the unusual billing of ". . . in creative association with Carl Sandburg." We gathered that Stevens had become quite fond of Sandburg, finding a kindred soul in the rough-hewn romantic poet. Stevens's description of their last meeting lingered in our minds as we took our leave of him on the street a few minutes later.*

A: I kept pretty close to Carl as he was getting old. He was always so vital. A man gets that old, people start to worry about him, but you never worried about Carl. When he was out here, we arranged that he would get up about ten and come in around noon; he loved to work late, he loved to go to parties. Anyway, I'd go see him at his home [Connemara Farm in Flat Rock, North Carolina] from time to time, and the winter he passed on, I went after not having been there for a year. We had some laughs; he was a wonderful man for laughter. When I bade him goodbye, he reached in his pocket and pulled out a piece of white rock. On it was written, "George, from Carl. A piece of the rock." The guy is poetic even with a chisel. Because that's the rock he has looked at out his window for the last forty years, a great big rock sitting out back. Anybody put a chisel in that, he would have brained him. So I was shook up. I said goodbye and started walking down the trail. I knew what he meant by that—it was farewell. The more I thought it over, I decided to take a look back. And as I self-consciously look back, he self-consciously looks over *his* shoulder to see if *I'm* looking back. He waved at me. Geez, I hated to see that man go.

Q: *That was the last time you saw him?*
A: Yeah. "A piece of the rock." People look at that and say, "Who's Carl, a bartender?"

INDEX

CONVERSATIONS WITH FILMMAKERS SERIES
PETER BRUNETTE, GENERAL EDITOR

The collected interviews with notable modern directors, including

Robert Aldrich • Pedro Almodóvar • Robert Altman • Theo Angelopolous • Bernardo Bertolucci • Jane Campion • Frank Capra • George Cuckor • Brian De Palma • Clint Eastwood • John Ford • Terry Gilliam • Jean-Luc-Godard • Peter Greenaway • Alfred Hitchcock • John Huston • Jim Jarmusch • Elia Kazan • Stanley Kubrick • Fritz Lang • Spike Lee • Mike Leigh • George Lucas • Michael Powell • Martin Ritt • Carlos Saura • John Sayles • Martin Scorsese • Steven Soderbergh • Steven Spielberg • Oliver Stone • Quentin Tarantino • Lars von Trier • Orson Welles • Billy Wilder • Zhang Yimou